Contents

THE AUTOBIOGRAPHY
OF A POET

Duncan Glen, September 1981. Photograph by Euan Duff.

THE AUTOBIOGRAPHY OF A POET

DUNCAN GLEN

THE RAMSAY HEAD PRESS   EDINBURGH

First published in 1986 by
The Ramsay Head Press
15 Gloucester Place
Edinburgh EH3 6EE

0902 859 854

309812

c c

Printed in Great Britain
by W. M. Bett Ltd, Tillicoultry

CHAPTER 1

Belonging

PERHAPS my first memory is of a very old lady dressed all in white, including a white bed cap, in a bed also all white and in a room again with all white walls and ceiling. I cannot have been much more than two as my sister was not yet born and my mother took me in my pram to visit this friend whose mother it was in the bed. I cried so much that the next time we went I was left downstairs (it was a flat on the top floor of an old cottage) in the garden. My mother always said it was because I was shy, but I well know it was because of that white old lady in the white bed in the white room. Some thirty years later I wrote a poem of that room. It appears in my long sequence *In Appearances* and reads:

THE ROOM

There's that mirk room I ken
Whaur she bides faceless, unkent;
A quate box-bed white wi her
I never kent but see again.

A shawl'd whiteness seen blin
Wi gruntin, soughin sounds
That turn me quick to that winnock
Daurk wi its hauf-drawn blin.

And on the waa the bress airm
O the licht is swung out
And mantles murmellin and lowin
Ahint globes I mind o as a bairn.

White waas that turn and rise to gie
A glisk o her I kent
Wha's face I canna see, and ne'er will
Though she bides for aye in me.

That room was in Cambuslang, Lanarkshire, in perhaps 1935 as I was born in January 1933. We had quite a way to go to visit my mother's friend as she lived well into Cambuslang and we lived in a small housing scheme in Westburn, some two miles away. The scheme was built in the early thirties, possibly to accommodate workers in Hallside steelworks which was just up the road. My father, John Kennedy Glen, worked there. He was on the staff, unlike his father,

7

whom I was named after, who had to face the furnaces each working day.
But my father had other problems, as I showed in a poem from 'A Sort
of Renewal' which is part of my long sequence *Realities Poems:*

XVIII

SIX-THIRTY A.M.

It's day shift and six thirty
and my faither still in bed
as if on the dole. But that's no his
escape. He's a lucky ane in safe staff job
wearin collar and tie
and polisht buits. Lucky at his hie-heid ane's
desk. But each Spring he taks to bed
and tremblin haunds and dizzy turns
and risin nausea and turnin tummy
as he tellt me lang efter. But then aa talk o heat
and cauld frae office to furnace
and back again. But still in bed
his books and papers are out and he's countin
countin, countin . . . I'm impressed
but ken nocht but toom words
stocktakin, orders, spare capacity . . .
And freendly visitors sayin
'Still I hear you're slack the nou.'
My mither says, 'His bluid has turnt to watter
wi the heat and the cauld'. And men
at the door:
'Ony chance o a job afore owre lang?'

Westburn was a working-class community but with sub-divisions.
There were the toffs or posh people like us who lived in privately
rented houses and there were the council house tenants who had come
from I knew not where but were part of a slum clearance. To some of
the 'toffs' they were 'the slummies' although my mother did not
approve of the term. Something of the life of our sub-community for us
children and some adults is shown in my long poem 'A Journey Past'
which was written as if from a train passing Westburn and Hallside and
Newton station, as indeed I often did between 1965 and 1978 on the
train from Preston to Glasgow.

VII

Mr Hamilton was special,
on constant day shift,
and Mr Clow on constant nichts
and needin quiet

to get his sleep.
Kick the can, hide and seek,
cigarette names and ither
cross-the-street gemms
not to mention straucht fi'baa
couldna be to his likin.
He'd much prefer you'd think
the quiet gemms
atween wee boys and wee girls
round the backs
but then he was Plymouth Brethren
for aa he was kent to hae been
drunk on Setterday nichts.
Maist, like my faither,
were on shifts,
day, back, and nicht in turn,
and big men like Mr Smith
that warked some great rollin machine
that took pouers o strength and
endurance
ayont the ordinary man
and earnt them big money
– and broken backs.

VIII

I can mind my faither on the nicht
shift and the special treat o a lit
fire on gettin up. But he was on the staff
and wore a collar and tie
for aa his buits and
the holes
brunt in his suit
that showed (to me)
the dangers o the place.
No that boys believe
in dangers
or kent the wecht o men
on your back
unemployed
and bosses further back
but mebbe mair real
(as nou I ken)
at heid office. Yet we were
toffs
and I wasnae allowed
to forget that
at hame

> and bluidy noses doun the street
> – which shows
> hou aa is relative!

This social sub-division was one divide. Another, perhaps more important to the imagination of a future poet, was that up the road was the steelworks and all its accompanying industrial waste and a little beyond that was the coal village of Newton with its small dark rows of miners' houses. But near to Newton and near to us in Westburn was the River Clyde with its green-pasture banks dotted with cows. Across the wide river was the industrial village of Carmyle but it could only be vaguely seen. Down-river was a power station and further down the poorer parts of Cambuslang and then Clydebridge steelworks and beyond that built-up and black Rutherglen, Dalmarnock and Glasgow. But up-river, with Newton tucked out of sight, was a pastoral Clyde, although old bings dotted the fields as they did Cambuslang-wards too. This meeting of country and industry I have found to be a fertile area for a poet's childhood. As I said in 'Follow! Follow! Follow!' which is part of *Realities Poems:*

> There the toun meets the country,
> cultivated naiture aside the effects o technology,
> and through it aa the river
> Clyde
> pastoral-lookin upstream and daurk industrial
> doun. A place like the tide's edge
> but mair human. There are pools whirlin
> round e'en in that daurk river
> and I see fish risin to set aff rings
> towards the bank. And us throwin stanes
> faur out to the depths o the middle. And yet
> aye the watters
> flowin doun to the sea.

And the Clyde also features in the poems of another of my sequences, *Buits and Wellies:*

LANDSCAPED

> There's kye unner the spreidin trees by the river
> and some up to their udders in the cool watter.
>
> The pasture's fresh and green. A scene
> for a Scottish Constable? Look round
> and there's a bing growein bigger. Look up
> and there's a slag heap in a steel warks.

The ferm land jist tap sile keepin
the rain aff them howkin ablow.

CLYDESIDE

We are harin doun to the Clyde for a dook.

It's a sicht to be seen.

Raggit jerseys no quite coverin
our skinny white backs or meetin
owre-lang short breeks.
Stockins lost in our wellies or runkled doun
at our ankles if we hae buits.

We shoo the coos hopin for a ride
or at least a laugh.

The fermer's got it in for us
kennin us for what we are.

It's aff wi the claes and into the Clyde.

Glasgow stares us in the face
and we gie it a smile kennin nae better.

I have always liked the final two lines of the second poem as I, indeed, like the description of these wild boys although I have to confess that it is not true of my own clothes although it is to that of some of my friends. The action, however, is true enough.

In addition to this meeting of country and industry around Westburn I had a further divide. My father's people, as I have said, were industrial steelworkers, but my mother's lived on a farm – really a piggery but in an old farm building set in rural Lanarkshire at Nerston, above Rutherglen and Glasgow and near East Kilbride which was then a small village and not the New Town of today. This second divide is also to be seen in my poetry, although perhaps the industrial working-class Lanarkshire predominated with regard to the first fifteen years of my life. But I spent happy days at Nerston with my grandfather, George Tennent, not least at family gatherings on New Year's Day as I write in 'Neerday'.

NEERDAY

It's neerday.
It's ane o'clock
and the dinner's set in the front dinin-room
used but aince a year. Juist faimily
for aince – and *aa* the faimily

as it has to be. E'en fowre great-grandparents
lookin doun on the scene frae the fireplace waa
immortalised in oils. A blazin log fire ablow the portraits
and grandfaither in his richtfu place
at the centre in his muckle chair brocht through
for the occasion. And mither and faither
there tae. We bairns are at sma side tables, I ken,
but nou I feel my place there at the big table.

And out on the front lawn wi snaw on the grund,
as maun be, and the driftin sound
o the auld Scots sangs frae the sittin room.
A muckle snawman soon made
and attacked wi snawbaas till we're
at each ither – aa my mony cousins
and my wee sister.

And sae it gaes on without end
– grandfaither large at the heid o his faimily.
Aa again in that warm dinin-room
and at that muckle table. And each haein
sucklin pig like my faither mindit
lang efter
when neerday at grandfaither's
was nae mair
– nor ony meal!

But that house and buildings and lands did remain a focus for me,
even if not so much for the whole family after my grandfather's death. I
sometimes went there after school when my uncle and aunt had inherited the house. Indeed I have written of my uncle, Andrew
Tennent, in a section of my *On Midsummer Evenin Merriest of Nichts?*:

I am saddened by memories. But joyfully ride again
chestnut pownies with shinin flanks. Ride through
the rollin green pastures of Lanarkshire in childhood's
Spring. And him that taught me there ahint.

I am mournin the passin of my happy past.
The slaw walk risin to a trot outwards
and the wud gallop back by the hedgeraws
and unner beeches' branches hingin owre.

I do not attend uncles' funerals
or seek out growein graveyairds
but I brush doun pownies again. And his airm
strong and largely-freckled moves wi mine.

Few of my Westburn contemporaries can have had that experience
of horse-riding or, indeed, of other truly country experiences I
describe in 'The Gullion' from *In Appearances:*

> I can mind the gullion
> ayont the midden and the auld Alvis.
>
> A can mind the ducks waddlin out the gate to dook.
> And Peter goose takin out his wives
> through the slap – hissin and streekin his neck.
> The gullion for cuttin nettles wi a scythe and whettin-stane
> – or bill or heuk nou I mind the words.
> And cuttin new gress for pownies owre in the field.
> And boontree canes – for bows and arrows.
> The gullion for takin out the powny on a halter
> for special grazin when it's dried out. The gullion
> for cuttin fails.
>
> I can mind the gullion wi the swings
> and muckle puddles for jumpin. And the stane dyke
> for settin up tin cans for shootin at
> wi a point two five – I think. And the speugies
> and stookies and craws – and blackies e'en.
> And waas to sclim to fields for shootin
> foxes – ae fox – and maukins and rats. And huntin
> out peeweep's eggs or stanein wasps' bike
> – and rinnin for the gullion.
>
> I can mind the gullion and aa the lans ayont.
> I went back   and fund
> a wee bit boggy grund.

Parts of where I lived as a boy were, of course, slum lands and
industrial waste land but really we were just on the edge of it – or so it
seems to me looking back. When I went into Cambuslang and turned
up the Hamilton Road towards Blantyre or down into the lower parts
of the town, I was not affected by the rows of dark tenements in their
rundown state although I knew that some of my classmates who lived
in these slums had a hard time. I wrote of one of them in *Buits and
Wellies:*

DIAGNOSIS

> Billy's got St Vitus Dance.
>
> It's no the fleas
> or the things in his hair
> the Doctor says.

Billy, I may say, went on to a place at Glasgow University and became a minister of the Church of Scotland.

So also when I walked towards the main entrance of Hallside steelworks I was not depressed by the dirt and decay of the works' buildings or the heavy smell of smoke and grime which attacked my innocent nostrils. The school I went to, West Coats, was in fact in the very prosperous middle-class part of Cambuslang – 'up the hill' as it was called. But I was never once in one of these 'grand' villas although some of my father's cousins lived there. The school I may say, as my poem on 'Billy' reveals, served the poorest as well as some of the 'up the hill' families of Cambuslang but only to the end of junior school when the prosperous children went on to fee-paying schools. Since then I've lived in middle-class suburbia for long spells and even spent over a year living in part of a very beautiful Georgian country house in England and when I go back to Westburn I discern a sense of neglect in our privately-rented scheme which I do not believe was there when I lived in Westburn. The gardens are much neglected whereas we and all our neighbours took a pride in keeping them neat and trim. I have written of my father's garden at Westburn in a poem addressed to Allen Ginsberg, the American beat poet, although, of course, as I hint in the poem, even today Ginsberg is something of an eccentric figure to me with my conventional life. The poem which is part of my long work *The State of Scotland*, 1983, reads:

I think of Allen Ginsberg
and his individual American
sunflouers.

Sunflouers I ne'er kent.
My faither grew flouers in daurkest
Lanarkshire. He grew chrysanthemums neatly
staked in straucht lines and sweet-peas
on canes in an iron frame. He grew
gypsophila to gae wi the sweet-peas in
a tall crystal vase. Daurkest
Lanarkshire so they say. Steelwarks
and their muckle chimneys wi raisable
lids heich to the lift. And daurk
sheds and slag-heaps and railwey
sidins and waste-lands piled owre wi decayin
rubbish ayont ony classification. And pits
wi growein bings and miners'
raws sma daurk black houses back to back. And dirty,
smelly burns risin faur unnergrund flowin
past. And yet the green fields aa

aroun and the river Clyde movin through
the pastures dottit wi kye.

But sunflouers I ne'er kent till
I moved to faur places
and mixed wi fremit folk.

And fremit still though I sit wi you, Allen Ginsberg,
unner the shade of an auld LMS steam
locomotive (or is it Southern Pacific?)
Sit and sicht them inside
aabody beautiful and gowden. And here tae
I see them growein into 'mad
black formal sunflowers in the sunset'.

Of course in my days in Westburn the 'slummies' neglected their gardens but I took that for granted.

But the Clyde is still there and the fields on its banks although minus the old bings which have been lorried away. Towards Cambuslang electricity technology has completely taken over a large field I remember full of pedigree Ayrshire cattle and the buildings of the dairy farm to which the cows belonged have been demolished and its arable fields have become a new waste land. My mother took me to that farm when I was very young to collect milk – I remember still the implements and the smell of the dairy. I remember also a maid in starched white apron answering the door and I was curious about a dark room with a stair of uncovered plain white wood that I could see behind her. What memories young children have, to judge by what I remember of my very young days. So I feel regret and anger at the destruction of that farm, and the demolition and removal of a few old bings which merged into a pastoral landscape seems a poor achievement to balance the loss of a working farm. But the general impression I have when I return is still not of great poverty or neglect. Probably I would not feel at home there now having been intellectualised and middle-classed, but I do not feel depressed by the community that is there or by the talk of the children I hear in the streets. Their language still sounds familiar to me and listening to them I feel again as I did when I was at one with their predecessors. They are what I was and can be again in imagination. Indeed I have written a verse in my poem 'Houses' from 'Days of Places' from *Realities Poems* of the house in Westburn where I was born and lived in until I was sixteen:

II

There are people livin in my houses.
Houses ne'er revisitit. No e'en the ane that's the first

and mebbe the maist abidin. No a house at aa in fact
but an upstairs flet. No a tenement but fowre to a block.
Inside lavatory and e'en a bath wi hot and cauld.
Twa bedrooms wi ane to me mysel, being the elder.
There were a neat fowre o us as a faimily.
The waas o that house were steel wi hidin roughcast on tap
– Tintoun as outsiders sneered. But aa the mair
respectable for that. The kirk twice on Sundays and drink
a fearsom obscenity kept out the house
wi the Council Houses a constant warnin doun the road.
The gairdens aa weill-kept wi railins in front
till taen aff for the war effort. A neat house
that maun still staun for aa the later houses
and me a son o that house.

As children we did not go into our friends houses very much although we did visit our relations a lot. On one occasion, however, I was invited into a house and it is an experience which has stuck so firmly in my mind that it became the basis for what critics consider to be one of my best poems.

TO THIS VERY DAY

We were invitit in frae the street
the blins were richt doun
and we'd been tellt wee Jean
was deid. We gaed up the peth
ticht in a group
wee boys and wee girls
thegither.

Inside it was daurk
and smellt a bit to me
for aa that I took it for grantit
– juist Mrs Smith's
and different frae our house
or ony I kent
for that maitter.

'This wey' we were tellt
and 'Quiet' for aa that naebody
was makin a sound.
Nearer the bed it was lichter,
somehou, and aa moved closer thegither
seein the clean white shape
on the bed.

I moved wi them towards it
though haudin further back in my mind

for aa I was only five
I kent I'd be keepin
my een ticht shut
and dae that still
to this very day.

As I have already shown by quotations, something of this part of
Lanarkshire life that I knew in the late thirties is to be found in my
sequence of poems *Buits and Wellies*. It is a mixture of the life of
Westburn and the poorer parts of Cambuslang. Glasgow also comes
into these poems as I worked there when I left school and, of course,
when younger I sometimes went there with my father and mother on a
Saturday; and, a little later on, with a young friend I went to football
matches at all the Glasgow senior grounds; but I leave all that for a
separate chapter. Other excursions I went on alone or with equally
young friends were to Glasgow's Kelvingrove Museum and Art
Gallery. Here we were lucky in that the No. 17 tram from Cambuslang
went right across Glasgow to the Museum's very doors. It was the
Museum that first interested me with its many models, stuffed animals,
armour and so on, but in a way the tram journey was as exciting as the
Museum. In *On Midsummer Evenin Merriest of Nichts?* I've written of
looking back and being again in that No. 17 tram which is, of course,
long gone from the streets of Cambuslang and Glasgow:

> Dreamers and poets and clowns
> upstairs in the No. 17 tram
> singin a daft, saft sang
> shooglin to where we are no sure.
> We hear the conductress
> 'come oan get aff'
> but we're steyin oan.
> The front's the back
> and the back's the front
> on this No. 17 tram
> shooglin us back the wey we've come.
> And I'm no sure if I'm dreamin
> or clownin
> or poet
> singin a sad, sad sang.

I may have been a twelve-year-old dreamer but certainly the idea of
being a poet never entered my wildest fantasies. It never occurred to
me that poets or poetry existed outside school books. But three or so
years later I was visiting the Kelvingrove Museum and Art Gallery for
the Gallery and not for the Museum. I had, quite uninfluenced by

anyone, discovered the Rembrandt – A Man in Armour – and the glorious collection of French paintings. How well I remember the first time I stood before that Rembrandt. I think this shows how a great work of art can make a strong impact on the young and unsophisticated. I've written of this Rembrandt several times in my poems and in a section from 'Follow! Follow! Follow!' the Glasgow trams also feature as images of 'thisness' – the essence. But what they stand for is best found in the poetry and not in second-hand prose:

> We staun
> at ane ayont ony thocht o knower and known
> in aa that's real. The last tram cams shooglin
> out to Pollokshaws bricht agin the wet nicht
> and grey tenements as that knight in shinin armour
> in Kelvingrove Art Galleries
> – a Rembrandt we say
> and cairrit round the warld as
> that reid wheelbarrow seen again
> clearly set in USA we'd imagine
> yet in reality here and onywhaur.

The red wheelbarrow is that of William Carlos Williams' famous poem which begins:

> So much depends
> upon
>
> a red wheel
> barrow

But it was many, many years before I discovered that poem although from an early age I had been a member of Cambuslang's public library, getting as many books out as often as I could. Each Cambuslang school had a day when it could take out books from the Junior Library and I used to ration my reading so that the books lasted the full week. Later on when I joined the adult library I got as many books as I wanted, and that was certainly a lot, although none of them was poetry. Later again when I was working in Glasgow I borrowed books from Glasgow Corporation's Stirling Library and I also joined Lewis's (the large store) Library where I got many, many novels. When I went to Lewis's in the late forties and early fifties there were queues to take books out – now there is no demand for such commercial lending libraries. At this time I also read in Glasgow's famous reference library, the Mitchell. How I envied the young men who worked there and that library features, as does the Glasgow Rembrandt, in a poem in which I describe taking my wife-to-be, with pride, around Glasgow. The poem is from 'Scotland's Hert' another part of *Realities Poems:*

IX

STRANGER IN TOUN

You being frae Fife and born in Mallaig
I took you to see my Glasgow. The warm
humanity o Argyle Street and the distinctive
smell o the Subway. The haill lang length
o Sauchiehall Street and a quick visit
to the Mitchell Library and my first seat o learnin
at the table near the back. I took you for a walk
on Glasgow Green and into the People's Palace.
We stood by Clyde at the Broomielaw
and I spoke o steamers for Doun the Watter
and happy holidays at the Fair.
We went on tramride to the Art Gallery
and I stood wi you afore Rembrandt's
A Man in Armour. We had time
to haud haunds lookin out to the country
frae the heichts o the University and stood
quait in the nave o the auld Cathedral. I showed
you Barlinnie Prison and the closes o daurkest Coucaddens
and the seikness o the Gorbals. We had a seat
in the sun in George Square wi its mony statues
and there was much Victoriana to be seen
afore high tea in famous Glasgow tea-room.
We had the best seats in Alhambra
Theatre for pantomime wi real Glasgow
comedians at the day's end.

Being frae Fife and born in Mallaig
you said
'I liked the Rembrandt.'

But I jump ahead and in my boyhood the real world for me was
Westburn and school in Cambuslang. Close life was part of my
Cambuslang and the first poem of *Buits and Wellies* has steelworkers
going home up closes although I was thinking of them coming home to
Westburn which has no closes. But it could as well be Cambuslang:

AFF THE NIGHT SHIFT

Wee grey men walk doun the street
without a word bein said. The sun's a reid glory
at the street end wi the Spring dawn brakin.

They turn up the closes
leavin reid dust frae their buits on the stairs.
He draps into a chair and stares at the out fire.

I had an aunt and uncle and many friends who did live in tenements and I knew the life well and played in the back courts. Thus we have my poem 'Dance' which is the final poem of *Buits and Wellies*. Before quoting the poem I should say that we were a proud working-class family with standards to maintain and my mother would never have let me wear wellingtons without toes or boots with flapping soles. But my description is typical of many friends I played with. Who the 'big fella' is I am not sure but I 'know' (hope) he is right in the context of the poem.

DANCE

Bairns are rinnin through the close
up the stairs and dreepin doun
and round and round again and again.

Lichts are bricht in aa the windaes
round and round on every side.
There's e'en a full moon high owreheid.

We are dancin on the wash-house roof
the taes out our wellies
and buits hae flappin soles.

Big Jean's got the wash-house key
and's in there wi her latest date
close up against the waa.

There's a big fella come out the close
laughin and lookin up at us
as the hail warld birls round and round.

CHAPTER 2

Innocence

MY CHILDHOOD days in Westburn were not only days of complete integration into a small community – of belonging – but also of innocence. A poem of mine which has been seen as truly expressing the life of the people and places of my working-class Lanarkshire childhood is indeed entitled 'Innocence'. It is from *In Appearances:*

In the days afore the war
The teas were the thing
At our house.
Kitchened mince collops
Wi doughbaas, and the breid
Soakit and sappy
In wattery gravy. Or black puddins
Horse-shoe anes tied wi a string
And made as only MacDonal*
Kent hou. Or the treat
O fried tatties kept frae
Dinner.
– And me but a gutsy loon.

In the days atween the wars
The teas were the thing
At our house.
Thin sheaves o fried breid
Brouned and crisp on
Baith sides.
Or jeelie-pieces; thick
Door-step anes wi the jam
Rinnin aff the marg.
And scones: tattie scones;
Soda scones; or treacle
Scones.
– And faither out o a job.

In the days afore the war
The teas were the thing
At our house.
Pancakes richt frae the girdle
And gane afore the butter
*Ramsay MacDonald & Co.

Richt haurdened.
And ginger-breid: 'Best without
Butter or cream'. And aye
A great joog o soor-dook
To gae wi it aa, frae the cairt
Comin special at fowre
O'clock.
– Wi mither in the queue.

In the days afore the war
The teas were the thing
At our house.
Cream cookies; braw sugar-tapped
Anes wi the cream oozed out
For lickin.
And biscuits to finish;
Perkins, bannocks mebbe,
And e'en the haurd Empire
Biscuits wi reid toories on
The icin.
– And me but a growein loon.

Ruth McQuillan has written of 'the very fine "Innocence" which catches for ever the flavour of a place and time as surely as Ramsay or Fergusson did'. And the Welsh critic Sam Adams wrote in *Anglo-Welsh Review* (No. 43, Autumn 1970) 'though it is little more than a list of traditional Scottish dishes, somehow he manages to convey an awareness of pressures of the thirties – unemployment, depression – together with a regret for all the good things unappreciated in the past but now longed for and unobtainable'. I do believe 'Innocence' is accurate as to the community we lived in in the late thirties, even if not completely so to our own family life. My father was never unemployed and neither were my immediate relations but many people in West-burn were and stood daily at the corner of the street. I would quote another poem from *Buits and Wellies:*

UNEMPLOYED

No yet at school
I'd watch them.

They stood at the corner
passin up an doun the street
at regular times.

I thocht it naitural.

Mebbe so did they
by then.

Until recently and the terrible return of widespread unemployment no-one even in industrial Lanarkshire expected the bad days of mass unemployment of the thirties to return, but the threat of unemployment has not been absent for long from the minds of the steelworkers of Lanarkshire – or from the minds of their wives. There have been threats at regular intervals to close both Cambuslang's Clydebridge steelworks and Motherwell's Ravenscraig which would put thousands of men out of work and affect all Lanarkshire. In 1975, when there was talk of closing down Hallside steelworks, I wrote a poem entitled 'John Kennedy, Steelwarker 1939-1975'. The name is part of my father's but he is not the man in the poem as he worked in Hallside 1916-1944 if I remember right. This poem is from 'Scotland's Hert' in *Realities Poems:*

VII

JOHN KENNEDY, STEELWARKER 1939-1975

The haill warld kens o Celtic Football Ground.
Pass it by. Pass through the grey canyons that are homes.

Suddenly you are at the warks. Clyde Iron Works
jined to Clydebridge Steel Works across the river
and the Foundry doun the road at Tollcross.

The warks o Parkheid, Tollcross, Carmyle and Cambuslang.

Ahint the black pouer o the warks aa would seem desolation,
filth and scrub and rubbish
– but here the tanner-baa helped build Celtic Park's fame.

A daurk Clyde meanders through
about to come to a stop in some underwarld, it seems.
Yet it has its pastures e'en in this depressed land.

A solitary carronade wi cannonbaa stuffed in its mouth
made to defend thae shores frae Napoleon
points out across the bosses' caur park.

Napoleon ne'er came, nor the Kaiser, nor Hitler.
Aa warked for you could say.

Nou aa's for scrap.

'You canna expect a job for ever', says John Kennedy.

There is also a reference to unemployment at the end of 'A Journey Past'; an ending which reveals my mixed feelings for the community of Westburn/Cambuslang and also my no doubt idealistic hopes for a better future:

I regret no being
or hae'n been a steelwarker
like my faither and grandfaither were.

Nostalgic nonsense
and yet the community is there
for aa to see and be a pairt o
for aa the slow decay o unemployment
aa the Hell ahint thae steel waas
wi their smells o heat and dirt.

But they hae to be made anew
as us – me – as weill
without the slavery to the common cause
o killin,
unnecessary Wark,
and to steel and to coal.
The Clyde can be pure again
wi licht flashin frae its blaeness
and a new green warld growein on its banks
in the bend o the river
and Clydebridge truly a brig.

Our Clyde atween Ryan Brig and Newton,
wi their historic warks and pits,
fresh in the smell o flouers
in a new Eden but wyce wi the knowledge
o the Hevin and Hell o needit
creative wark
and o peacefu, tyaavin thocht!

As I have said, none of my immediate relations suffered unemployment and, indeed, at least one of my aunts was said to 'have money'. Certainly she was always opening small businesses, although not very successfully I deduced from family talk. She features in one of my *Buits and Wellies* poems although, when I wrote it, I could not quite remember what she used in the pancakes to save butter as well as guaranteeing an equal rise in all the products. I remember it as turpentine but I am open to correction:

AUNT JEANIE

My aunt Jeanie had a baker's shop.
I had the idea she put turpentine in the pancakes
for economy's sake.

For sure she needed mice to keep the cats doun.

This particular aunt also moved house every other week, or so it seemed to the child that was me. They were all rather run-down one-room-and-kitchen houses, which was perhaps why she 'had money'. Her husband was also a great changer of jobs and even took off to faraway foreign London at one time. He also had the distinction, frowned upon by most members of the family, and certainly by my tee-total mother, of going into pubs. But he was not ostracised by his relatives, being part of the close-knit family – not least when we went on holidays as I demonstrate in another *Buits and Wellies* poem, although the crowded arrangements were in reality only to meet an accommodation emergency. I hope Cousin George's humour in this poem will appeal as much to the outsider as it did to the family at that time.

FAMILY GROUP

We were close as a faimily
though no unusually sae.

There are photos wi twenty-six o us
at Millport for the Fair.

The landladies aye thought we had a lot o early visitors.

Wance we had a house richt on the front.
Up a stair. Nae single end but twa rooms.
A single bed in the back ane for granny
as weill as the cooker. There was a waa-bed
in the front room that took six. Even so
cousin George said he had to staun up to turn round
sleepin on the flair.

Aaready he'd forgotten what it wis like
in a single end.

But we did not always go on holiday with the Glens; sometimes we went with my mother's folk and then we lived in considerably greater style. We even one year had a famous Scot with us – Johnnie McGrory, then British and British Empire boxing champion. My uncle Robert Tennent was friendly with McGrory. I've written a poem on two memories I have of Johnnie McGrory – a 'proper wee gentleman' was how my mother remembered him when she read my poem. Not many people can claim to have given him an uppercut as I did when a young lad. But the poem reads:

TWA MEMORIES

I can mind when Johnnie McGrory
cam to stey at our house
when I was juist a loon.
It was at our holiday house
at Kilchattan Bay
and Johnnie slept
in a box bed.
I've aye had it in mind
that he was ill and indeed had come
to die – a second Benny Lynch.
I'm tellt nou by a visitin uncle
– McGrory's second in his great days –
that I've got it aa wrang:
Johnnie was juist on holiday
like everyane else.

But I can mind
a feart loon being gien
a boxin lesson by Johnnie McGrory
at grandfaither's funeral.

That was, of course, my mother's father, but the granny in 'Family Group' was my father's mother, Mary Glen, although she had become a grandparent quite early, comparatively, and preferred to be called grandma. She lived to nearly ninety and well into my adult life, but I remember her best when we visited her on Sundays as children. I've written of her in *Mr & Mrs J. L. Stoddart at Home:*

You led a vegetable life as lang as I kent you.
I can mind you aye
aside the fire but alane. Grandfaither
lang deid. A sma daurk wuman wi
white hair. A stool at your side. And on the stool
twa bibles. You read them continuously – your only
readin. You didna talk muckle to me
– or onieane. Nor gied me sweets.
Or e'en advice. You ne'er touched me
so faur as I ken and for sure
ne'er kissed me or showed onie affection.
Nor me you. You cooked nae meals for me
though you washed up the dishes till the end.
You did naething for me that I mind
except gie me a quick look if I misbehaved.

You were not withdrawn, though neither,
obviously, were you freendly. You juist
took me (and yoursel) for granted.

And I luve you still . . .

My maternal grandmother died almost before my memory but, as
'Two Memories' perhaps suggests and as I have already said, I remember my maternal grandfather well and have written quite a lot of him.
Perhaps most powerfully in *On Midsummer Evenin Merriest of Nichts?*
just before he died:

A bed's been made for him,
my grandfaither,
in a dounstairs room
next to the bothie. A room
wi nae proper purpose
till nou.

But the bothie through the door
ahint the Chinese-petterned draught-screen
is a place for mony purposes.
The bothie in name
but nou a wunnerland
for aa ages.
Boxes upon boxes o toys o mony aunts and uncles.
And muckle rockin-horse heich as the powny in the
field
if no sae fat. And a lockt press
wi the guns imagined though shut out o sicht.
And the saiddles and the reins and martingales
and bits. And mony kinds o whips. Whips wi knots
for crackin and whips for ridin.
And a bench wi raws and raws o tins.
o nails and screws. And mony tools hung
on the waa. Mell and haimmer,
aix and saw. And in the corner
a free-staunin airn fire wi black lum
raxin to the roof. And near it sticks for kindlin
and clog wi ither aix stuck in it.
And skippin-raips and punch-bag
and muscle-developers owre stiff to streetch. Aince
this was a gym wi ring for the trainin
o anither Benny Lynch to be. On the back o the door
to the stable (nou a gairage)

a dairt board. And a fox's brush
on that door leadin back into the house.

But nou he's through there
in that toom room.

I'm caa'd in to his bedside
but he's gien up talkin
– for lang his greatest pleisure . . .

CHAPTER 3

'Follow! Follow!'

I COULD have left school at fourteen – one of the last with that 'opportunity' – but I stayed on, only to leave at fifteen much against my mother's wishes. I went to work as an office boy in a large Glasgow printers with the intention of becoming an apprentice compositor which I eventually did, although only after happy days as one of several office boys in the company. There is a poem in *Buits and Wellies* on these happy, innocent days in Glasgow:

TWA FEET IN EDEN?

I'm fifteen
and near dancin alang Maxwell Street
I gie a feet-clappin jump owre a stank and
about burst out laughin.

It's the first mornin o my first job.
Junior clerk but maistly message boy.

I've done a wee test and got them aa richt
but wan. I tellt him I was richt in that tae.
He laughed and tellt me
'You are the highest ever.'

I am clerkin at a high desk o my ain
wi ink and pens. Day books, order books,
work sheets, and round the warks
chasin jobs.

I'm paid twenty-four and six a week.

Soon I'm promoted again.
I'm near to twenty and still
dancin alang Maxwell Street.

Nou I ken it must hae been Hell that Eden.
Edwin Muir has tellt us.

In fact I did not remain in that office, or indeed in Glasgow, until I was twenty.

Edwin Muir gave one of his books the title *One Foot in Eden* and he worked in several offices in Glasgow, and the Glasgow area, which he found very uncongenial. I expect I would have found working in the stinking bone-factory unpleasant but the, no doubt, unsympathetic thought occurs to me that Muir was at least in the office and not in the actual yard or factory amongst the stinking bones. Anyway, I was happy in my Glasgow office and did not find Glasgow at all depressing, unlike Muir who was, of course, comparing it with his 'Eden' of Orkney. But Cambuslang and Glasgow were my Eden, or my first Eden as an Eden can occur at any time in one's life if you have the right attitude or response. Mine may seem a strange Eden as seen in poems I have already quoted or as described in this extract from 'Follow! Follow! Follow!' from *Realities Poems:*

> They would hae us believe in the beauty
> o the heich hills o naitur
> but there's my Lanarkshire
> wi its warks and pits and bings and railways.
> Its wee fibaa grounds
> and close-livin folk. Aa
> dismissed as a waste land. And yet staunin on
> an auld bing and seein the tall lums o the warks
> daurk agin the evenin lift
> is capable o disturbin me
> wi elevatit thochts.
> A sense sublime, indeed!
> and lang afore I'd stood on ony heich hill
> or heard o Tintern Abbey.

Amongst many other things 'Follow! Follow! Follow!' is about Glasgow football and in the section quoted above I refer to the 'wee fibaa grounds'. These are the grounds of junior teams and mine was Cambuslang Rangers who played at Sommerville Park. From the age of ten or eleven I was very involved in this game of football, although since I went to the RAF in 1956 I have considered myself free of it; or free until I was asked to review in 1976 *We'll Support You Evermore. The Impertinent Saga of Scottish 'Fitba'*, edited by Ian Archer and Trevor Royle. This book brought back to me all the myths and the magic of the Scottish gemm. In it I found recreated some of my own heroes and the many heroes of the contributors who also become our heroes in the reading. As a poem by Donald Campbell says in its final lines: 'My Bauld/and My Wardhaugh/an My Conn', these being, of course, Tynecastle heroes – Hearts. Alan Bold is also a poet but contributes an essay to this book. His heroes are the 'famous five' (sounds a bit like Enid Blyton) of Hibernian 1949-55. For the uninitiated the famous five are Gordon Smith, Bobby Johnstone, Lawrie Reilly, Eddie Turnbull and Willie Ormond. For Alan Bold from his seventh to his thirteenth year going to Easter Road was a 'blessed release' from what he describes as 'an unspeakably dull world'. He is on the side of young people living now in a similarly deprived world. He writes: 'Today when football supporters are widely execrated for their violent enthusiasms I condemn not them – but the appalling domestic, educational and social environment that makes football all there is to live for, the one bright light in a blank, dark space. Because if there is nothing else then there is nothing like following a great team that is both exciting and successful. In such circumstances football becomes not so much a substitute for life as the quintessence of life itself.'

I am less forgiving of the violence in these young people in that my generation was equally deprived but much less violent. But I know well what Alan Bold is talking about and his words must strike a chord in many people's memories. With me, as I have said, to start with it was the wee Rangers of Cambuslang, and then very soon, the big Rangers and Ibrox Park. As to heroes, for me there is Torry Gillick at inside forward elegantly slipping the ball out to Willie Waddell of the dashing long stride, powerful cut in on goal and the final unstoppable shot into the back of the net. Or the superb cross for the polished head of Willie Thornton to nod the ball into the net. There was also the fact that Willie Waddell had one new bootlace for every match. But, like going to the Kelvingrove Museum, the journeys to and from the match were almost as important as the game itself. At a very young age we were going right across Glasgow from Cambuslang to Ibrox. I am amazed at the knowledge we had of the routes to and from the ground – and all the other Glasgow grounds. Tram, train or subway, we knew them all and which was best in relation to movement of the crowd leaving the ground. This feeling of belonging to a big, happy crowd as we walked to get the tram or subway is something unforgettable once experienced without affection. I've written of this experience in 'Follow! Follow! Follow!':

I've shoutit wi the best o them at Ibrox
and merched for the train hame
wi pride and warmth in my hert
as hundreds walkin wi me.
I wouldna claim great things for
the experience but there it is. And wuds
and meadows lie by the Clyde
in that barren daurkness
as we're tellt
and frae that green land
squeezed in aside the warks

and seepin slums
mony can raise thochts o *their* truest soul
as frae grey streets whaur gemms were played
as real and true as ony on green playin-fields
whaur white flannels
mak a pretty picture. Aa for
real
if without a thocht o
self-
expression.

The same poem also expresses joy in the actual game and the reliving of it in talk, although I think I regret that this talk is not usually raised to a recorded art form. The second line of the poem refers to the 'striker'; in my day he would have been the centre-forward:

The wee Man's jiggin round the defender
and the striker waiting by the post. The goalie
poised to leap and gresp
and aa wi their een on the baa
as the haill croud. A movin
minute aa action
and truly taen for itsel
as the baa hits the back o the net
and aa is uproar
and joy
– for the moment.

And re-lived in talk aa week
till the next gemm.

Images o their reality if no gien heicher
form as William Wordsworth mindin the speerit
that moved him in the meadows and the woods
and the mountains and aa that he beheld,
frae an earth
specifically green.

As I got older I became a bit of a quiet rebel or outsider and I found a successful top-dog team like Rangers no longer to my taste. I went to the other extreme and became a supporter of the team of lost causes – Third Lanark. It was the era of wee Jimmy Mason and in him we have a heroic inside forward to put beside Torry Gillick and all the other unforgettable inside forwards. A whole host of them, from the great club men to the real immortals – the Jameses, Steels, Walkers, Baxters, Whites and McPhails. I am now demonstrating, as Hugh

Taylor said in *We'll Support You Evermore*, 'If you think there's nothing I like better than rolling these great names off my lips you're right'.

But as well as individual heroes there are great matches and great teams. One of the greatest teams in Scottish football history must be the Celtic one which won the European Cup in 1967, although by then I had lost interest in football, or so I thought. There are now many apocryphal stories of the night Celtic won. There is the one of a hitch-hiker stopping a car outside Lisbon, asking the driver where he was going and on being told 'Edinburgh' stepping aside and saying, 'That's nae use, I'm going to Glasgow'. But for me it is emotionally summed up by a few words spoken by Bill Shankly, Scottish manager of Liverpool, to Jock Stein, manager of Celtic, immediately after the game, 'John, you're immortal'. Note that 'John', a whole critical essay could be written on that usage.

I had my share of big games. Wee boys being passed over heads and bottles coming flying over, and yet (stupidly) we felt no fear. Not that we were foolhardy and, indeed, we were very safety-conscious, having at the big non-ticket games at Hampden, for instance, a safe stance immediately behind a path which went round the ground. With crush barriers immediately behind us we were not only in a very safe position but could also see very well despite our small stature. Not that we should forget the crudities of attending a big match even in the less violent days of my youth. I have described a little of this in two contrasting verses in another *Buits and Wellies* poem:

REALISM FRAE HAMPDEN PARK

'I came, I saw. I heard.
A roar so strong, so vehement, so feral.
A people gone wild in natural hate and joy.
A wild, strong, desperate and ebullient crowd.
An education in obscenities.
The Scot seen in his natural state
and never seen the same again.'

Jimmy naiturally opens his flies efter much drink taen
and the posh yin's shoes washed by a yella stream
he didnae ken enough to side-step.

Not that we boys were in the least offended by the language or the lavatorial uses the terraces were publicly put to by many 'Jimmys'. They were just part of an accepted way of life. But I would have been horrified to hear my father swear at home, although my mother used to say he swore at the men in the steelworks – so she had been told!

Alan Sharp, the novelist, contributes a most interesting essay to *We'll Support you Evermore* which includes the disturbing suggestion that perhaps in the World Cup in 1974 we were glad 'to find a good way to lose and not some means of winning'. 'If one considers Baxter's game, and if folklore is your thing, then it will be clear that Scotsmen value things in this world far above success, or integrity or intelligence. What they value most is what Baxter had, they value the completely held conviction of their own superiority.' If Alan Sharp is right, and he certainly makes me think, and we can see ourselves ritually enacted as a people on the football field, then this is a book worth studying even by those with no interest in football but who want to know more about the Scots in all their natural complexity.

After my time as office boy/junior clerk I moved to the reading room of the same printers. There I acted as copy-holder to the proof-readers, which meant reading the copy aloud to them. But I did learn the art and particularities of good copy preparation and proof reading which has stood me in good stead ever since. There is more than one way of getting an education. In the cramped quarters of that reading room we boy copy-holders had to let off steam somehow and I did it by becoming an argumentative talker. I had been quite a silent, though strong-willed, youth until then but there I learnt the art of argument and debate which I have enjoyed ever since.

Soon, however, I started my 'time' or apprenticeship as a composi-tor. Being an apprentice with relationships to journeymen is a dis-tinctive if not unique experience and one I am glad to have had. I truly felt part of a close-knit working community and took great pride in craftsmanship and in maintaining the standards of the firm. It was a company which expected loyalty from its employees and acceptance of its paternalism. But the immediate community of the composing room is what I now remember with most pleasure. Each man or apprentice was allocated a 'frame' to work at and how proud I was of mine, keeping it in very good order and well stocked with all the equipment necessary to a compositor. As is only to be expected, I've written a poem about it.

THE APPRENTICE

I hae been beaten doun to the grun
I would staun up for mair
the men movin around in daurk aprons
and me comin back at him again.

I was taen for mysel and kent
my place. Aa could pit me there.

I was the Youngest Apprentice
and naething comes lower nor that
yet I had my place and my frame
I felt at hame
a pairt o the place, yet mysel.

I was three frames frae the door
richt across frae the foreman
at his desk wi aa the jobs
eatin peppermints
attendin to the air-conditionin fan
lookin owre his specs and watchin the Baltic door
sittin on his hie stool near to God himsel
wi sod aa to dae though kennin
aa there was to ken
as I would, yet, mysel.

Naebody stoppt to think it out
though aa kent their pairt as I mine
we kent I kent my place
and soon would be in theirs,
at least, in due time.
I meant to gae back and see him
that knocked me doun sae weill
but like me he'll be thinkin
afore he speaks
to fremit folk even if it's, yet, oursel.

CHAPTER 4

Wha's like us? Here's tae us!

WE SCOTS are, of course, rather fond of looking at ourselves. Like many another nation no doubt we are fond of thinking no-one can quite equal us whilst at the same time attacking everyone whose faither we kent. Still, as Tennyson said, 'The man's the best cosmopolite/Who loves his native country best.' Although G. K. Chesterton wrote in his 'French and English', 'All good men are international. Nearly all bad men are cosmopolitan. If we are to be international we must be national.' And as the learned Samuel Johnson said, or so Boswell said he said, 'Every man has a lurking wish to appear considerable in his native place.' And of course Walter Scott cried in *The Lay of the Last Minstrel*, 'Breathes there the man, with soul so dead,/Who never to himself hath said/This is my own, my native land!' But Byron said of Scotland, his half homeland, 'A land of meanness, sophistry and lust'. Which some Scots might consider a compliment! But in making jokes we have to remember that to some people, and certainly to Sydney Smith as quoted by Lady Holland in her *Memoir* of 1855 (I elaborate thus so that no-one thinks it Sydney *Goodsir* Smith): 'It requires a surgical operation to get a joke well into a Scotch understanding.' But at least there are a good few of us scattered around the world so that the world may have its joke: 'There was once a Scotchman – and now there are millions of the bastards.' And *of course*, as T. W. H. Crosland said, 'After illicit love and flaring drunkenness, nothing appeals so much to Scotch sentiment as having been born in the gutter.'

But as the old 'enemy', Doctor Johnson, said, 'A Scotchman must be a very sturdy moralist who does not love Scotland better than truth'. But surely we are united in agreeing with Faujas de Saint-Fond: 'In general the women display an elegance and agility in their gait, and many of them have charming persons.' Of course he was writing only of *Glasgow* women! And Edward Burt wrote: 'Glasgow is, to outward appearance, the prettiest and most uniform town that I ever saw, and I believe there is nothing like it in Britain.' Being parochial, and ignoring Liverpool etc, we might say, with anger, that the last phrase remains true today! Glasgow is now the most socially deprived city in Britain. So let us hope the international dialogue continues, or starts, as must the national, although for the latter we have really no choice.

CHAPTER 5

Eyes to See

I HAVE begun this book with fond memories of the Glasgow area and by implication praising it or at least its social communities. But in the last chapter I suggested that Glasgow is uniquely bad, with regard to social conditions, in Great Britain – that there is 'nothing like it in Britain'. Yeats said somewhere that 'Nothing is ever persecuted but the intellect, though it is never persecuted under its own name'. One of the ways in which the intellect is persecuted is by having masses of people living in poverty and exceedingly poor social conditions. By depriving people of even basically good social conditions we are, with regard to the mass of these people, depriving them of the opportunity to climb up even the first rung of the ladder of truly civilised thought – as everyone knows, their intellects do not get the opportunity to develop as they could. I believe that we should not put poetry before the destruction of the social evils that lie heavy on many Scottish communities. Nevertheless those of us who are poets can perhaps fight these evils best through creative writing, although I do not suggest that poets have an obligation to write directly on social matters – the poet has to go his own creative way and no-one (including society at large) has the right to tell him what to write. His duty as a caring citizen is another matter.

Whilst living in Penwortham, Lancashire, from 1965 to 1978, I went quite often to Edinburgh, but mostly to attend literary meetings and to spend time in the company of literary people who, despite any personal deprivations, are a privileged group of people. I also went to Skelmorlie, Ayrshire, to visit my parents and to the East Neuk of Fife on holiday – both prosperous areas at least to the eyes of a visitor. I also revisited Cambuslang which has been given a new look with most of the old slums demolished. My Westburn remained much as it was in my childhood, if a little more neglected as I have already said. Not that I was blind to the industrial wastelands although, the now cleaned-up Cambuslang, of course, did not seem too bad. But I was invited to go to another part of the industrial West of Scotland to give a poetry reading and I got a shock. I had received a slight jolt a year or so before when in one of my visits to Glasgow I had walked along Sauchiehall Street and been depressed by its terrible state – there was a mini-fairground on one part of the street and all seemed to be in a state of decline. But I

37

thought that perhaps it was only temporary and that when the street was given its facelift it might not be too bad – not that I have much faith in town planners, as anyone who reads my *Clydesdale* poem can find out. This sad deterioration of Sauchiehall Street, and indeed the continuing depression of the Parliamentary Road area and other parts along the bus route to Cambuslang, occasionally nagged at my mind but I had not had a sharp enough blow to shake my unthinking acceptance that things were not any worse in my native West of Scotland than they were in parts of Lancashire where I then lived. Not that I was unaware intellectually of there perhaps being nothing like Glasgow for the social deprivation of so many, many people. Nor was I uncritical of the post-war planners or rulers of Glasgow, as a poem in 'Scotland's Hert' in *Realities Poems* shows:

VIII
GLASGOW PROBLEMS

I will tak you by bus to Easterhouse.

On the waste lands o this outer estate they gether
ane by ane on the pavements each kennin his place.
Every day they're there rain or shine in the gear.
Lads and lassies gettin younger it seems
each year. Maistly without a word
kickin their heels
passin the lang endless times o day and nicht.
A Glasgow gang.

In the city centre the starlings come swirling owre
as the daurk sets in. A fleshin cloud turnin sherp angles
on itsel again and again
agin the sky bricht to the west. Yet each
individual in its co-ordinations
and seekin soon a personal perch for the nicht
on daurk important offices and civic buildings.
They hae plans to scare them aff. Saft plastic,
or some such, on the ledges
gien a sense o insecurity.

A Glasgow gang. Passin endless time day efter day
till the action sterts. A question o territory.
The weapons out, faces slashed
and the buit pit in.

A pool o reidness left on a grey street
but soon washed awa and the street cleaned up.

The white drappins is the trouble for the City Fathers
– and in the business hert o the City.

But it was not until I went to give the poetry reading I have referred to that I really came face to face with the other aspect of Scotland – the hinterland of Glasgow and the industrial West: the dirt, the boarded-up shops, more dirt, the obvious poverty, the neglect at a social level, the frequency of stotting men walking the streets and not infrequent side-steppings to avoid dried – or not so dried – vomit. There were a few bright spots in this poverty-stricken grey land: one a library, an excellent Victorian building, very finely and sensitively modernised without destroying the character of the interior decoration of the original building. But then I stepped out into the dark, grey streets and my lifted heart sank to my boots again. Now, there were mitigating circumstances; it was a very wet, grey day after a wonderful spell of blue skies and golden sunshine in Penwortham, Preston, Lancashire, with its tree-lined avenues. I had been spoiled, but that perhaps let me see my native West of Scotland for what it truly is. And a sunny day might have made the depression and dirt and boarded windows and drunkenness and poverty even worse.

My first reaction to this evidence of social decay was sadness and depression but soon – very soon – this was replaced by anger. My thought was that the people should not accept such conditions, and by the people I mean those who pass through the worse streets to live in better ones, as well as the poor who live in the slums. Somehow they should rise up and say . . . What can they say? 'Look at us.' 'We are human beings too.' 'We deserve better than this.' 'We *demand* better than this.' But there should be no need for them to say anything. Anyone with eyes to see must be aware of the continuing decay of these streets. Someone should do something, I kept thinking; and then I thought, what would *I* do? What *could* I do if I lived here? How could I make my sadness and anger felt? How could I do something to change and improve? A little improvement I suppose would be better than nothing, but our rulers should not be let off the hook that easily. Radical change is what is demanded. Then I thought that no doubt I would gradually get used to the environment and cease to see the dirt and decay and ever-present signs of poverty, a poverty somehow worse at a community level than at a personal one with people often so bravely fighting the conditions.

This failure to see the places for real – as they really are – is obviously part of the reason why the people (the prosperous perhaps more so than the poor) do not demand change and refuse to have their community treated as a tenth-rate one, or a hundredth-rate one compared with the prosperous south-east of England. And I write 'treated' with due thought. If Lancashire, where I lived and which is thought by many Scots and, indeed, throughout the UK, as a poor blighted area of

Britain, is generally so much more prosperous than the Glasgow area then it is the responsibility of government to give the West of Scotland a deal as good as that given to Preston, say. Of course, there are parts of Liverpool and Manchester just as bad as any I saw in the West of Scotland but they seem to be in patches and not whole communities.

I do not underestimate the problem of wiping out some of the worst social conditions in Europe, or even just a weariness of spirit in the people, but one thing is certain, there is no need for investigating committees or a Royal Commission or any of the delaying tactics of a do-nothing bureaucracy. The problem is well enough known to those with the will to bring change. They should be given their heads on a grand scale – and given vast sums of money even if it means taxing the better-off. I am not against taxes; they are a means of achieving social improvement and nowhere in Europe is that required more than in parts of the industrial West of Scotland. The conditions have destroyed the moral and social judgments of some of the people but what is so reassuring about human dignity is how many of them retain their standards of right and wrong. The middle-class may not approve of the husband in my poem 'Lady, Lady' from *Buits and Wellies*, but perhaps the poem should stand without any patronising comment:

LADY, LADY

There dwelt a man in Babylon Lady, Lady.
SHAKESPEARE

There bidit a man in Glasgow
lady, lady.
He was weill-kent for his weekly shauchle
doun to the broo. His lady, lady
pushed a pram to the steamy
and skelpt the bairns
out onto the street.

He came hame, seik on the stairs
and shoved her on the bed
aside the bairns. She took
what she got
lady, lady.

As I have said, a sense of community can survive even the most trying social conditions, as can loyalty to family for long beyond the concepts, it seems, of social or town planners who have been responsible for huge desolate housing estates and demoralising high-rise flats. But let another of my *Buits and Wellies* poems speak for itself:

CONSIDERATIONS

We've aye bidit up this close.

The room's sodden, seepin, thick wi slime
and grime. There's the rats at nicht
and the bairns hae to be watcht.
We hae to watch oursels.
A bite can soon gae septic.

The sanitry man says we should tak
the new council house. Upstairs still
but wi a stair o our ain. An inside lavvy.
In fact a bathroom. It would be grand
but what about granny.

She's been here aa her merrit days.
It wis her house
afore ours
and she has a say.

I like to think that in some of the poems of my *Buits and Wellies* I have
caught the will of many, many people to maintain their standards of
decency against the odds; and also, indeed, in another sequence,
Spoiled for Choice, in which I tried to give Glasgow and the industrial
West a voice in reply to some of the more pompous statements made
by American poets, whom I admire but send up in these poems. My
own favourite amongst these poems is:

XVI

ARGUMENT

for inspection 'imaginary gardens with real toads in them'
MARIANNE MOORE

I tell ye I saw it, a fox in the back gairden
            wi big broun tail
    sittin up eatin a nut frae the tree
            at the tap o the gairden.

But, hen, you couldna
    there's nae tree at the tap o the gairden.

Hou dae you ken I couldna . . .
            Ye ken fine,
                    there's nae gairden!

There is plenty of courage shown and true kindness can be found in
the most unexpected circumstances, as I try to reveal in one of my

'Traivellin Man' poems from *Realities Poems* which is by way of a back-handed compliment to the warm-hearted if sometimes violent and certainly socially deprived and neglected city of Glasgow which I left with regret in my late teens. In the poem I am returning to Glasgow after a long absence and have come from Preston, Lancashire, where I was living. I am no longer an accepted Glasgow man but someone to be asked 'Whaur are you from?' But let the poem speak for itself:

X

THE HERT O THE CITY

In Glasgow, that damned sprawling evil town
G. S. FRASER

I'm juist passin through
late at nicht. I risk a walk doun
through the gloomy tiled tunnel o Central Station
to Argyle Street and the Hielantman's Umbrella
for auld time's sake.

I see them at aince. Three girls and a wee fella
wi a bleedin heid. He's shakin wi laughter
and the bluid's splatterin on the shop windae.

I'm juist about awa back up the stairs when they're
aa round me. 'On your ain?' 'It's awfu cauld!'
'Ye shouldna be here by yersel!'

I canna help but notice the smell o drink and dirt.
His heid's a terrible sicht.

I looked round but I *am* on my ain.
'Whaur are you from?' 'Preston?' 'You'll know Blackpool?'
Soon he'll hae my haill life story out o me.

'You maun be cauld' and
'Ye shouldna be here by yersel.'

I offer them some money to get in out o the cauld
but they laugh at the idea. They're no hungry
and there's plenty wine left.

They'll get fixed up themorrow.
It's warm enough unner the brig.

They'd walk me back safe to my pletform
but the polis'll be in the station.

'Ye shouldna be here by yersel!'

CHAPTER 6

Magic Places

My FATHER left the steelworks after some thirty years – in, I think, 1944 but he had been trying for some years before that to get out and had dreams of buying a house with land and greenhouses to run as a nursery or market garden. I wrote a poem about this entitled 'Open Lands' which is part of 'Days and Places' from *Realities Poems:*

My faither had dreams to tak us to a life in the country.
We visit weill-biggit stane houses set in acres o land.
We would live there when arrangements could be made
and faither out the happt waas o the steel-warks for guid.

My faither saw raws and raws o multi-colourt chrysanthemums
and dahlias. He felt the warmth o the sile in simmer
and touched tomato leaves in gless-houses for their fresh smell.
Mither would feed some hens and geese be our watchdogs.

We would be free on that rich warm land. And dinner
taen thegither afore a log fire in that stane house.
Nae mair piece-boxes and stewed tea in a steel-warks
whaur warm fires meant dirt and sweat and auld-age afore your time.

I had dreams juist as strong if vague and insubstantial.
Great explorations to be made and new warlds fund
through thick wuds and alang green peths to rinnin burns.
Aa in an endless simmer and continuin play taen for grantit.

Nou I hae a house biggit o English brick. A neat suburban gairden.
There's trees line our boundary and a burn tae
but nae real warm land to wark nor hens nor geese
to feed. My bairns ken nocht o the talk o steel-warks.

My faither had dreams o life in the country
and land to wark unner blue skies and in clean fresh air.
Land to pass to us in time. I listen
and dream wi him o thae ever-open lands.

In fact when my father did leave the steelworks for health reasons he went to work for my uncle, Andrew Tennent, on what had been my grandfather's piggery, but after a few years he took another job and we moved from Westburn, Lanarkshire, to a house situated in the foot-hills of the Campsie Hills, Stirlingshire, which lie only a few miles north of Glasgow. I continued to work in the Reading Room of the printers in Glasgow, walking each morning down a rough track and along a country road lined with smallholdings to catch a bus to the city. I was sixteen and took to walking the hills each evening on the light nights and at weekends. Walking and climbing these hills made a very strong and lasting impression on my imagination. The first poems I ever wrote were based on memories of walking up the side of a burn high on the steep face of the hill above our house. The part of the burn I saw in my mind's eye as I wrote my first poems is quite high on the face of the hill but the full length of the part of that burn which was familiar to me starts from a country road and passes through rough land and a gorge and hill pasture land and then moves onto the face of the hill. This route is a strong image in my mind, rather as the Langfall above Langholm was important to 'the groundplan and pattern' of Hugh MacDiarmid's mind. One of the first realised poems I wrote became part of a slightly longer section of *In Appearances*. The poem is entitled 'De Profundis':

> Here. Here on the heich hill
> the yowe is lean
> and leanin.
> Aye thinner, sparer;
> the exposin banes and holed een
> days o decay aside
> the drainin burn.
>
> There. There the loch is fat and swalt.
> The flashy skin o lallan sloth.
> The sun reflects on the surface gloss
> but ablow
> the mindin depths.
>
> The burn calm frae the peat
> braks doun on the stanes
> and the skull o the yowe;
> the dam is strang
> the watter feeds easy
> to the loch.
>
> A cloudit loch fat and lown
> wi edges feedin the sheep;
> ablow the drains are strang
> and fremit watter
> feeds easy to the toun
> and foul
> to the sea.
>
> And cloudit hills are lang and grey green
> and heavy wi bog.

It seems like yesterday instead of many years ago that I walked these hills and I can still see clearly that dead sheep beside the burn. But it was quite a few years later, in 1972, that I wrote the poem which describes realistically, although with other layers of meaning I hope, the length of that burn from hill-top to river. It is entitled 'Watters' but the first word is 'Burniebrae' which is the actual name on Ordnance Survey maps of that section of the Campsies:

WATTERS

Burniebrae; whaur the watters flow o'er
and are white
       wi fechtin and strivin,
the dams directin to safe reservoirs; but the burn
still survives the dams to run through fields and pastures.

The twistin watter scars the green fields
wi nou broun watter flowin quaintly
      whair hill-fairmers walk
and orange-stained sheep graze; and in
the enclosin wud, sherp-edged rocks
turn the watter again to white.
      Low in the gorge the watter roars
and they that wad see hae to sclim up
afore the watter turns peacefu again in lowland fields.

Watter drapped doun frae heich hills to be met
      by addle watters
frae the piggery owre the hill, coverin the stanes
wi slime; muck that kills yet feeds; slime
that is lost as the burn turns to the tributary river
in a lallan village –
      till fouled by the pulp mill's watters.
Movin slowly on to the toun and doun to the womb
o the movin Clyde alive wi the hoot o horns
      and ships movin doun to the sea.

When one climbs to the top of the seen hills above our house one comes to a large flat area of rough dull green grass. Before reaching this moorland there are, if one stays close to the burn, rocks to be climbed and I've described this in 'The Image' which is part of 'Ane to Anither', yet another section of *Realities Poems:*

I stert to sclim the rocks aside the faa
and am Mallory on Everest
strivin because it's there. I pull up owre the tap
and there's my reward. Nae heich peaks

risin to the lift or blue lochs atween lower bens.
Course flet gress streetchin on and on
and a cauld wund I can haurdly staun agin.

I tak in the flet desolation
wi the grey sky seen as faur as the dull gress
and the aince livin burn nou sma, flet and nairrow at my
fit. I staun astride it
nae bother. And bog cotton round muckle holes
like bomb craters frae the blitz o my childhood
but less human.

Each individual picture complete in my heid
and yet somehou projectit in the air
in a space afore my een
– seein image that is idea.

But if one walks forward across that rather desolate plateau, as I did after a few weeks of exploration sideways about the tops, one gets a surprise. A pointed peak suddenly appears ahead and a fine 'mountain' it is. It is named 'The Meikle Bin' or the large ben or hill. One of my poems, in *In Appearances*, has that title although it is about the journey down the face of the hill above our house. It is also, of course, about different ways of seeing reality and about the creative process or imaginative heights and levels as indeed is 'Ane to Anither' which critics have seen as strongly metaphysical below the straight-seeming description.

THE MEIKLE BIN

In the hauf licht doun frae the Meikle Bin
aa is clear and boundered round;
the dour daurk thorns are licht years awa
wi the gloamin starns nae faurer
than thae trees but a step doun, and me
anither warld awa frae them
and me to you
I think but a hunner fit ahin.

But no for lang. My step is doun
and round the merchless path
to nicht . . . and day . . .
and bourached figures on a knock.

But the foothills too are very important – or at least were to me – although the thoughts of the final poem, 'Then Shall I Know', of *Realities Poems* are the thoughts of the poet I became long after and not of the youth who walked these Campsie Hills. Certainly my thoughts were inarticulated then.

I

I would return to the magic places o my youth.
Tak you on burnside walk by fithills o Campsies
and the heich hills of innocence. Aa
taen for real without a thocht o leid.

II

I see mysel a youthfu sixteen
walkin alane by the burnside.
Step efter step through the lang gress
and stoopin as needit ablow the trees
hinging owre. The gress bends to my step
and I tak a wey through there
as if a landscape made for me
though pethless and boggy in pairts.

There's the quick rustle o birds aneath the bushes
and mavis's sang shairp frae a branch
heich and daurk agin the blue sky.
And through the cuttin o the burn
suddenly the heich hills
kent in their richtfu place
frae mony lang walks
yet nou moved close in
but a step ayont that nearest linn.

The cheyngin flow o the burn, the quait breeze,
bendin blade o gress and gethered greenness
a diversity o single wunner
shairp and clear. And a warmth aa round
taen as pairt o this weill-kent place.
And silence tae as mavis flees aff,
but soon it, or ither, in full sang frae heicher branch
and juist as naiturally true.

Step efter step and een and ears
and aa that is that youth
in taen perfect harmony as that that is
aa around. Aa perfect to that single youth
and in its richtfu place
as he thocht
and walkt at ane wi it
joyfu in the kennin wunner
– though thinkin aa ayont him
tae.

III

Look back to the stane in mid-stream,
the faaen tree, the fence to be sclimed
and honeysuckle smellt. The hundrit-leggit
beast and the bricht-colourt fungi on the tree.
Look to the face o the heich hill
and white hillside burn flowin owre. The linn
to be stood ahint and rainbows seen.
And rocks to be sclimed to the tap.
The cottage by the burn wi reekin lum,
and ferm set doun low wi shelterin trees
at back. Look to hill-fermer walkin
his mony acres. And his dugs warkin the sheep.

Aa taen then as equal
ayont ony conflict
– and aa circlin round me!

But now I hae shown it to you
and you to me anew
as real as you
lit by the licht o our luve

– and aa the warld in it . . .

CHAPTER 7

Sangs of Joy

WE LIVED for only a year on the Campsies but I shall always be grateful for that year. It is doubtful if I could have written *In Appearances* but for the images given to my mind and my imagination at the impressionable age of sixteen or seventeen. In a review of *In Appearances* in *Akros* 16 (April 1971) John C. Weston saw me using images of the Highlands and the Lowlands to shape my book and continued: 'The Highlands represent the poet's mystical, contemplative, universal, timeless, silent aspects; the Lowlands represent his responsible, everyday, noisy, changing aspects.' Leonard Mason in his long analysis of *In Appearances* in his book *Two Younger Poets: Duncan Glen and Donald Campbell* analyses the high hill situation of the poem very shrewdly, I think, seeing the poet/speaker 'down from the Meikle Bin (the apex of creativity or the Hill of Paradise) throughout the book and in the reverie or in-between state when the attempt is made to understand (and to communicate) the knowledge gained at the height of creativity. It is still a heightened state of understanding and well above the everyday world but not the topmost moment when the act of creation takes place.' Mason's analysis of the high hill aspects of *In Appearances* is too complex to comment on here but later in his essay, when discussing my book *Gaitherings* he suggests that the poem 'Reality', originally printed in *Feres*, 1971, could be 'the poet thinking of where he took us and what he did in *In Appearances*. It is also a description of all creative artists worth their bread and cheese, although there is also the realistic situation and the humour of real outdoor lovers. The Duncan Glen humour is very much in evidence.'

REALITY

I hae taen you
on the heich hills.

I lauch as time gaes out wi
you and I.

I ken it aa.
Or think
 I did
 – ayont ony leid.

49

Reality?

Nou reason's kickin back.
I hae thochts
– and they are lookin owre their shouthers.

Time's come back.

There's a cauld wund on my dowp
and I'm feart what folk'll see
o you
or
me.

But my use of the high hills in my poetry does not end with *In Appearances* or, indeed, with images drawn from my Campsie days. I have climbed many other hills since then. High hills feature quite markedly in my *Realities Poems*, 1980, including sections of joy or praise in 'The Inextinguishable' which show that I still associate the high hills with creative acts. I quote one of these sections:

I sing a sang o joy. I sing of man heich
on the heichest ben of creation. Man
ane
in the sang made perfect for his time.
I sing of the burn
pourin owre the hillside brae. The burn
pourin owre the langest linn
and a singleness reflectit
in the deep pool ablow
openin up warlds anew.
I sing of the path alang the edge atween
inaccessible peaks. And seein aa around
frae meadow to heichest ben. And the wund
through my hair
and mind open to the sky seen
endless blue
and lochs and bens on and on
and on ayont ony end in sicht.

I sing of man alane wi joy that is
in being. Himsel upricht and facin
himsel and what was and is
across his thocht. The thocht
constructit and made haill. Aa
birlin round
as twa luvers thegither
as ane.

Our being opened out
for itsel, alive and rich in luve
deep in oursels
thegither. I sing sing sing
I sing wi the young mavis in the meadow
and the laverock risin free free in the air
abune the hieichest ben.
I sing wi the young luver
ploughin straucht across a field
and his wife seen turnin hay
in simmer by heilant lochside.

And cottage wi reek at its lum
and aa the warld passin by
it thinks. But themsels
true to themsels and a warld creatit
time and again in circle upon circle.
The noblest circle as she bends
owre the hay and their son in pram
by the field's edge. I sing o her and him
and us and them in gowden years
celebratin our joy ane to anither
and kennin we are daein it tae
in our humanness. And yet
a richer fullness there
ayont ony thocht unnerstaunin.

CHAPTER 8

Into the Sun

WHEN my parents left the Campsies for Fife I lived for about a year with a widowed aunt, Isabel Coghill, and her son, George, in Giffnock, an affluent suburb to the south of Glasgow. But at weekends I went through to Fife – to a farm cottage near the small village of Star, near Markinch which is about nine miles inland from Kirkcaldy. Many years later I wrote a none too complimentary poem on Star village as part of the sequence 'Traivellin Man' from *Realities Poems*. I'm told the village is now a place of commuters as well as true country folk but the poem is accurate enough of when I lived near it.

XVI

COUNTRY PLACE

Gin a body kiss a body,
Need the warld ken?
ROBERT BURNS

I'm revisitin the langest village in Scotland.

You can smell the pigs frae ane end to the ither
though it maun be about twa mile in length
twistin mair nor links o Forth. There canna be
fifty adult folk bide here
but bairns aawhaur
and mony no quite aa there.

There're wells by the side o the road
and at gloamin time a lad can be seen cairryin twa pails
frae frame and ropes across his shouders.

Like Jill's Jack

There's nae hill to sclim or pub to sit in,
nae kirk to perform the needit ceremonies.
Nae gas or electricity. There's the village haa
presentit by the lady laird
and the Post Office has near aa you'd want.

Still you'd wunner whit is done to pass the time
till you think on
thae simple lads and lassies.

52

Whilst living on the Campsies I had learned to fly-fish for trout and during the fishing season I spent most of my weekends in Fife fishing Carriston reservoir. I caught little but enjoyed the activity of casting and hoping, as do all anglers worthy of the name. I was rather lonely during the week in Glasgow and it was at this time that I began to read what might be termed 'serious' books and to educate myself.

Soon, however, I had transferred my articles of apprenticeship to a printing firm in Kirkcaldy in Fife and I was living with my parents in the farm cottage up the hill from Star village. My father was the pigman on Carriston Farm, looking after a pedigree herd of the now-rare Tamworths. He took pigs to all the major agricultural shows of Scotland and England and his office was most colourfully, and proudly, wallpapered with rosettes.

I've described my walk (actually I often cycled) from Carriston to Markinch and bus journey to Kirkcaldy in one of the poems of the sequence 'Walkin in Fife', another part of *Realities Poems:*

III
STARRY TALK

I walked the road frae Carriston to Markinch
aa the year round but think
o being up at six-thirty on daurk winter mornins
and doun the road wi a newspaper unner my coat to keep out
the cauld. I jog dounhill to Star and its twistin road
heavy wi the smells o the wee ferms. And owre
Cuinin Hill through the bracken and doun the track
to unner the michty railwey brig. A quick run up to
St Drostan's kirk and sprint alang Markinch's High Street
for the bus to Kirkcaldy
whaur I wark echt to five-thirty.

And you bidin at the end o the High Street
unkent to me for several years to come.

And the same jog at nicht waitin for the first time
when it'll be licht when I get hame. But nou I mind
the evenin star green to the richt as I walk up
the last streetch frae Star village. Venus
in her green silk goun
o later years. But afore that I ken you
and we gae out thae roads and talk o starry maitters
still jinin us thegither in walks o joy.

The 'you' who lived at the end of the High Street was Margaret, my wife-to-be, but it was a few years before I met her and started walking the roads of Fife with her as described (sometimes with poetic licence) in 'Walkin in Fife'. But my first year or so in Fife was not a happy one. I was not accepted into the community of my new firm as I was from Glasgow and I did not help acceptance by forming an arrogant belief that the composing standards of my fellow craftsmen – journeymen as well as apprentices – were lower than mine as established by my old Glasgow company. I was an arrogant but worried, depressed and lonely young man who saw his future gone in this new inferior (as I saw it) job. I turned in on myself, to reading and to writing short stories, even to planning a novel. Indeed I made a start on it but my imagination ran wild and I lost control of it as, indeed, happened several times over the years when I attempted novels. Eventually, though, in the middle seventies, I did take firm control of my imagination and wrote a rather realistic one. It was rejected by all the publishers I sent it to.

This introspective year or so in my life was perhaps useful to me as a future writer as I not only began to write but also to read extensively in all the great novels – English, Russian, French. My wife sometimes tells me I can be very self-absorbed and no doubt I am when I am writing a long poem or in the gestation period before a poem. However I do not think that I am self-centred, but if I am to some extent it is not an attitude of mind that I really approve of – although certainly a poet has to look inwards to himself as well as outwards to life. In *In Appearances* is a poem entitled "I am" which is about this looking at oneself. I intended it to be something of a horrific poem and while some people have certainly responded to it as such others seem to have had doubts as to its emotive or emotional power. It was the first of many of my poems that Nat Scammacca, who later edited *La Nuova Poesia Scozzese* with me, chose to translate into Italian but Alastair Mackie wrote in *Akros* 33 (April 1977): 'The self-absorbed inspection of the reflecting ego as subject and object is as austere as its language; further comment seems unnecessary. It's a stance Glen is drawn to but I find its nudity chilly and chilling.' To which I cannot resist commenting that this was exactly my intention. But let the poem speak for itself:

'I AM'

'I am'

I hae a little voice that says
'I am'

I hae a little voice that says 'I am'

I hae a louder voice that says
'You are'
to me

I hae a voice that says
I am
my sel
lookin at my sel
lockt in a wee room
lookin at mysel

and there's nae door out
that wee wee room

'I am'
'I am'
'I am'

'I am'

Although I had discovered Hugh MacDiarmid and bought some of his books whilst living in Glasgow, I did not write poetry until much later. Soon, however, I threw off my depression and there followed a very happy and uncomplicated few years when I was a haunter of dance halls with a group of male friends, and also a friend to quite a few girls. There is a dance section in 'John Atman' in *In Appearances*. Alexander Scott kindly told me that the second part of 'John Atman', from which the following quotation comes, was the best description of male adolescence years that he had ever read.

And the dance. Heids on a hidden
floor. A turnin licht movin
through the spectrum. The warm
wi the cool. A sad yellow
and a turnin green. Heild ticht
on sprung boards. Turn and turn
again. The great springs taut
in ithers' haunds.

Great gaitherings o dochters
turnin. The owre-lookin.
And the dance. Close and fast
turnin steps. Time and time again
round movin limbs. Quick steps
and slaw movements. Gyrations
full and round wi the beat
time and time again.

Tall slow steps; quick turnin
heids and quait talk. And the hame-
takin
by the sea.

> The sea against the stanes.
> A breakwatter ablow the street
> And large steps unner watter
> black and live wi the broken
> lichts
> stretchin across the bay
> calm ayont the risin stane,
> sand banks and crustit rocks.

On these evenings at dance halls male companionship was also
important, as I said in 'John Atman':

> Great journeys taen across
> ither fields open to ither lichts;
> great doins imagined
> and fulfilled in acts o talk.
> We walk out loudly in
> saft shoes
> scornin the sea
> and the lang-legged dochters;
> a time for lauchter and nonsense
> and great facts in rough houses
> staunin against the sea.

But soon I met my wife-to-be and walked her out on the roads of
Fife. We also spent a lot of time dancing in Kirkcaldy. This was the
time of the big dance bands and they all came to Kirkcaldy Ice Rink.
But another attraction of Kirkcaldy, although only once a year, was
the Links Market which stretched the whole long length of the prom-
enade of the Lang Toun. My 'Traivellin Man' sequence has a poem on
the Market:

XV

BY THE SEA

I had a luve walked by the sea

SYDNEY GOODSIR SMITH

We're back in the Lang Toun for the Links Market
for our bairns, we say.

I mind takin you aince a year
in our courtin days. An annual celebration
we walked haund in haund the haill lang length
and were on aathing.

The steamboats near swingin richt owre
and the dive-bombers daein juist that. The dodgems

to show what a deevil I was at the wheel
haein nae caur to drive you hame. And elaborate
new-fangled stomach-turners
nou forgotten. I shot an air-gun at wee pipes being
a crack-shot and threw
pingpong baas into gold-fish bowls nae bother at aa.
We bought candy floss and hot dogs
and rolled pennies doun wee slides
till aa our money was gone.
Still we *were* laden wi prizes!

Prizes soon forgotten as we walked by the sea
and stood close thegither in the daurk
doun by the sea-waa.

Nou the bairns canna be kept back. I face the horror
o the steamboat but aince, and disgrace mysel
being seik ahint a caravan. I'm grounded.
I dinna quite live up to my Buffalo Bill image
and I suspect the hot-dog stall to be unhygienic.
Still I'm a whizz-kid on the dodgems
and I can cairry aa the prizes the bairns are winnin.
The trouble is their money disnae seem to be runnin out
and we'll be back themorrow nicht.

They can cairry their ain prizes.
Wan thing husnae cheynged
– we can still walk by the sea!

I also took my future wife onto the hills, including the Lomonds of
Fife, the Campsies and Ben Lomond. I cannot say that she took to the
hills like a duck to water. She did not really care for getting her shoes
muddy or her feet wet – and still does not. But she learned, as I've
written in the first poem of 'Ane to Anither' from *Realities Poems:*

I

LUVE

I've aye been keen on the heich hills.
It was naitural I took you, my luve, to the hills.

You saw nae reason for them,
or us, being
there. Glaur and wet and mair wet in burns
to be crossed. Wund and cauld
and caulder and wundier at the tap. And mist
and ae fit in front o the ither
for langer than you'd thocht possible.
I was the deil and wud wi' it
– and ne'er again!

> But come the sun and days by the burn
> heich on the hill. I'll ne'er forget
> the lawn-like gress
> in a giant's armchair o rock by the langest linn.
> And your first real tap. The view o the lands ablow
> and the peaks and the lochs to the West.
> I see you there still
> silent, apairt and yet us thegither
> beautiful.
> I've lang wondered if God felt
> like me or you like
> God.
>
> I've aye been interestit in God!

Looking back I still find it surprising how someone comes out of the unknown into one's life and before you know where you are all your old ways are abandoned as if they had never been and certainly as they had never been given up for previous girlfriends. As I was to write in 'Seeven A.M.' part of 'A Sort of Renewal' again from *Realities Poems:*

> It is Spring and seeven in the mornin.
> Haund in haund in the sun doun the street
> and he's there my auld freend
> across the road. Oh,
> where are my freends of auld?
> Whaur the Friday nichts in mony baurs?
> The Setterdays at wild dance haas
> and mornins at billiards and serious male talk
> ony time, makin new the warld? My freends
> are gone into a warld o licht that blins
> them out. You're come
> but a movement o a girl
> and we cross nae street
> but walk thegither into the sun.

Not that serious courting, as everyone knows, is all joy. Indeed sometimes there is a kind of hate as well as love as I wrote in part of *On Midsummer Evenin Merriest of Nichts?:*

> Frae tree to tree, frae beech to beech,
> Aheid you walk alane in the cool shade.
> It's made for luvers, I think, this green glade.
> 'I hate you!' is said in your every stride
> But here I decide I'll bide.
> I'll pick a flouer to show wha's in charge
> And look up at the sun and the warld at large.
> But, I think, soon you'll be ayont my reach.

I run and walk, and run, and walk by your side.
I hope the gesture will get through thick hide,
I've my pride for aa I ken your hate's frae luve.
I'll juist touch your waist. I'm no sma mysel!
In time you'll turn and rise abune yoursel
Though hate, I ken fits a luver like a glove!

But generally these were very happy days, as have been those that
followed although naturally there were quarrels later as in our courting
days. My *Mr & Mrs J.L. Stoddart at Home* takes the form of a married
man looking back and to the future as well as being in his now which
contains all these thoughts:

I sing of heich hills, of flouers, licht and waddins
of wuds, brigs, of you and your daurk een.
I sing of us thegither, nicht walks, haunds, lips,
of ither things ayont our ken but us oursels.
I pit my trust in you, sang and luve thegither,
wi leid and touch and movements
we tak wi the words risin to our lips unaskt
and taen for themsels
and ayont our daily sels . . .

we can anerlie dream
efterwards
and turn to us, as ane, again
for the licht

I sing of earlier days, of nichts, walks in wuds
and crossin brigs haund in haund,
of you and your daurk een
lookin, wi kennin glance, at me
lookin at you. Of nichts as I
hae thochts rinnin frae me
to sing to you, as you are
and as you'll be . . .

Nichts bricht wi your licht but there's times
I hae fears o fleein time
wi you (or me!) alane. The daurk
draps doun and I turn wi cauld
to shut een, fauldit haunds,
and a face whiter than onie new-bleached sheets
– mine? or yours? I wouldna ken!

But the nicht is the same
– you or me! –
for aa I ken it comes to aa
and brings forth the same tears.

Aye, indeed,
the joys o luve are mixt wi tears
lang afore the physical end.
Wi luve, it seems, maun gae hate
such are the strang emotions we hae
and yet the forgiveness is the luve
and our weys jined for themorrow
as the licht wins out again.

I would walk you out through the wuds
and count the starns owreheid in a black nicht
that is bright for us. We can talk
as we walk in our ain warld without a thocht
o past or future. Aa taen as it is the nou
and for itsel. And by day flouers growein wild
allround and reid squirrels
lowpin frae branch to branch
abune our heids
and yet a pairt o us for the nou
and for aa the time we hae.

I sing of us thegither, of heich hills, brigs and green banks,
of flouers, licht and daurk, haunds and lips.
I sing of wuds, of you and your daurk-haired beauty.
Of our time thegither and our dance bit by bit
if I kent hou
takin it complete
and for itsel
                    in us . . .

I would dance you out
as for yoursel

I would dance you haund in haund
owre and owre again
                    to your tune
                    quick eneuch for baith . . .

CHAPTER 9

Walking in Fife

IN THE last chapter I briefly referred to walking the roads of Fife whilst courting my wife-to-be. I have already quoted one of the poems from the section of *Realities Poems* entitled 'Walkin in Fife'. This sequence describes, with some poetic licence as I have said, this time of our lives. The whole of 'Walkin in Fife' was printed in the magazine *Words* which was edited by Carl MacDougall and published from a Markinch address. This printing gave my work quite a popularity in Fife which pleased me a lot. Two of my poems were reprinted in the house journal of Tullis Russell the Markinch papermakers and following upon this they asked me for more Fife poems and I wrote one entitled 'Memories' specially for them. But here I would print some of the poems from 'Walkin in Fife'.

I

STARS AND HOULETS AND SQUIRRELS

We are out haund in haund on the back road
by Viewforth Plantation on the streetch doun
to Newton Farm. We look at the stars sae bricht
and I name what I ken. You are richt surprised,
the sky at nicht on country walks in winter
being new to you. Later, I say, there'll be
aurora borealis a saftness across the sky
and you're e'en mair surprised though you've lived
for years in Markinch toun,
but a mile or sae frae here, simmer and winter.

I draw on the furthest extent o my astral knowledge
and risk my airm round your waist
though it's only our second walk out thegither.
The stars are bricht owreheid and we tak the road
doun by Newton Farm and ancient terraces and Stob Cross
and Markinch the Pictish capital o Fife.
But these are daytime places and you were
no impressed as I try anither knowledgeable tack.

Still there's the houlets and squirrels in Balbirnie woods
e'en if I tried to show you them
on our first time walkin out thegither!

61

VIII

WINTER PEAK

You couldna believe your een
kennin it every day frae anither side.

Me walkin you out on a bricht December day
wi snaw to be struggled through
doun to the Mill Deans Road
and alang the straucht streetch to Rameldry
and the clear view to the West.

There as if by magic lantern or carpet it rose
as we steppt clear o the trees. It lookt baith distant
and as if we could touch it in the dry clean air.
Its outline sae sherp and risin white to the blue sky.
A seemin Alpine giant wi knife-edge ridges and shadowed face
suggestin baith heicht and depth.
A real Matterhorn set doun in pastoral Fife.

You couldna believe your een
and held me close at the wunner o it,
and nae words to speak . . .

IX

THOCHTS

Only three miles but seemin like ten,
You and I out for a Sunday walk in our courtin days
and takin the straucht wey hame across the fields
frae Teuchat Head.

Frozen stubble haurd and ruttit aneath our feet
and the cauld a waa to be faced
and bravely walked through. The quait December air
enclosin stillness aa round but for the crunch o frost
aneath our feet. Haund in haund we lean furrit
and think only o the end o this walk
and escape frae that cauld,
we thocht. Haunds sculptured lumps without feelin
and noses cauld ayont ony pain.

The nicht is closin in fast for aa the brichtenin hoar
and aheid the sma lichts o Burnside show we've faur to gae.
But soon doun by the watterman's cottage
and the tall windaes of Carriston House our next goal
bricht owre the reservoir unseen ahint its bank
but felt in a cheynge o air. Nou roun by the loch's faur edge
and large dovecot agin the Western sky. And Lomond Hill

a white Matterhorn aa day nou a distant greyness
and ither warld. We think on a sma cottage
and blazin fire, and escape frae this cauld,
we thocht.

Nou I mind the walk frae Teuchat Head to hame
and you out walkin wi me.

X

KEEN

You thocht we should hae a lang walk on Sunday.
On Setterday we had sclimed East Lomond frae Falkland
and walked the taps to West Lomond and then back
hame by Leslie, Markinch and Star
a very, very twistin village.

On Sunday we set out by Drummy Wood whaur we stoppt
the walk no being aa for courtin couple. But soon
doun the steep brae wi muckle laughter by East Forthar
and West Forthar and a wee stop in the hay loft.
And airm and airm into Freuchie on its quaitest sabbath
but wi a kirkyaird we could doucely walk round.
In Freuchie we ate our sandwiches.

On out the road to Newton o Falkland and Falkland itsel.
We hae sclimed the Lomonds yesterday
but you want to revisit large copper beech
in the wud aneath the hill. I forget my tiredness
at the beech but mind it on the lang, lang road.
to Markinch by Kirkforthar Feus
and Balbirnie Estate whaur I revive a little
on a seat aneath anither famous beech. You lead me
up and owre Cuinin Hill and through twistin Star
a very, very lang village,
and up the hill wi the evenin star green to our richt.

At nicht you talk o a walk out to Drummy Wood
in the daurk
but I took to bed for a week
– alane and exhaustit!

XI

TWA STORIES

We went to St Monans
and you raved about the herbour and the kirk

and I tellt you o Buckhine* wi its ideal herbour
and the fishin-folk and their close-set houses
doun to the herbour and round the gowden bay.
I tellt you o sandy beaches pairt o the glory
o Fife. I relatit stories o the Dutch settlin
Buckhine in the sixteenth century
and aa the tradition o the place.

You said we must gae but I tellt you
o mines being sunk and sea-coal
piled heich on the gowden beaches
and o an infilled herbour
and empty fisher-folks' houses.

You didnae speak to me aa the wey hame.

XII

THE UNKENT

Late at nicht we come owre the Cuinin Hill
through the trees closin in, and out by the tinkers' camp
wi daurk bulbous tents and tethered horses.
We walk very quaitly close thegither but fast
at the sound o their howlin and wailin that's mebbe
singin. And the stirrin o horses.
The stars are bricht in a daurk black sky
and the moon castin lang hidin shadows. Feelin
the nip in the air and that singin gettin nearer
we set aff into a slaw tip-toe run
haund in haund past their tents. Quicker and
quicker but as quaitly as we can wi quick looks back
owre our shouders. The singing cheynges key
as we turn onto the main road
and the sound o our feet loud as drums
but there's nae thocht o stoppin wi the deil at our heels.
Weill past nou we laugh and are aff into a happy run thegither
doun into Star village wi its daurk windaes
and the neighin o grey mare aside North Dalginch farm
and soos gruntin in Bellfield's sties close to the road.
A stoat or weasel's quick across the road
and houlets hoot in the nicht air.

But what we ken
– at haund!

*Buckhaven

XIII

TRULY CERES

You wantit a lang and truly rural walk.

I reeled aff Mill Deans to Coaltown of Burnturk
to Claybrigs to Cults and Pitlessie Lime Warks
to Paradise Farm and Chance Inn and finally Ceres famed aa
owre Fife. The maist rural walk in Fife I said
and endin in its prettiest village. You made
me tak you to prove me a deceiver and found three cottages
lackin aa mod cons at Mill Deans, seeven cottages
at Coaltown o Burnturk wi the only coal that for their grates.
And Claybrigs truly an ideal ferm wi pure spring watter
at its gates. The Lime Warks gied a blot it's true
but David Wilkie was born in Cults and made Pitlessie
Fair famous to become limner to the King.
I near made Paradise at its ferm
but you wantit to push on to the Chance. A disappointment
to find a wee hamlet o cottages but still raisin up
imaginins o the auld coachin days.
And to Ceres needin nae words wi famous green
and brig and Bannockburn gemms played there still.

I hae thochts on ither gemms
and you aa woman there in Ceres.

But you (delichtit wi the pleisure I'd gien you
walkin frae Mill Deans to Ceres)
truly woman, said to me, 'Mill Deans and Coaltown
of Burnturk and Claybrigs and Cults and Pitlessie
Lime Warks,
– you tried to trick me out o it!'

XIV

THE SHORTEST WALK

We hae walkt mony roads o Fife thegither.
A courtin couple wi mair to walks than walkin
or talkin. Our langest walk by Drummy Wood
and doun the steep brae to East and West Forthar
and to Freuchie and out to Newton o Falkland
and to Falkland itsel and the fithills o Lomond.
And the lang, lang road to Markinch
by Kirkforthar and Balbirnie Estate. And up owre
Cuinin Hill and through twistin Star
a very, very lang village
and up the hill wi the evenin star green to our richt.

And our last courtin walk. To a seat unner a copper beech
in Balbirnie Estate and out alang the back road
to Viewforth Plantation and the streetch doun
by Newton Farm whaur the stars are bricht
in the black January sky. And back round by
St Drostan's and alang Markinch High Street
to the end whaur you bide till themorrow efternoon . . .

Themorrow at fowre you'll tak a short walk to meet me
staunin afore the Reverend Davidson o St Drostan's Kirk

and that walk mindit as the langest
by Drummy Wood and East and West Forthar
and to Freuchie and . . .
                                        on and on . . .

CHAPTER 10

'A Labour of Love'

DURING the later part of my time at Carriston with my parents I was attending Edinburgh College of Art on a part-time basis and in my last year there I was awarded a full-time Andrew Grant scholarship for one year. I lived in digs in Marchmont in Edinburgh, although I went home at weekends to see my future wife – we became engaged on 28th December 1955. It was at this time that I became involved with the work and ideas of Hugh MacDiarmid although, as I have said, I had read some of his work before that.

I left school ignorant of Scottish literature but in my days at my aunt's in Giffnock I read a lot of popular Scottish novels by writers such as Neil Munro, Eric Linklater and George Blake. I did not take to the works of Neil Gunn and, indeed, I still retain a prejudice against his work which is no doubt a fault in my response to an important novelist within a Scottish context. I also read quite a lot of Walter Scott's novels; I did not read his poetry and the only Burns I remember reading – and this earlier at school – was 'The Cotter's Saturday Night' which I had no time for and which put me off Burns for many years. Although ignorant of the native Scottish cultural traditions I was something of a natural Scottish nationalist and I began to read Scottish history books, including what I thought was the history of Scottish literature – in other words Henry Grey Graham's *Scottish Men of Letters in the Eighteenth Century* which I admired a lot, accepting quite naturally that Scottish literature was a part of English literature. I still have a notebook in which at this time I listed the important figures of English literature – they were all novelists from Richardson to Virginia Woolf. The only Scots in the list are Smollett, Scott and Stevenson. As I have said, I was at that time writing short stories and contemplating a novel. Very soon after that I discovered modern Scottish literature through, I think, buying the Saltire pamphlet *Modern Scottish Literature* by J. M. Reid. I wrote out a list of Scottish writers beginning with Macpherson (Ossian) and Sir Walter Scott and ending with Sydney Goodsir Smith. As I already said, I had read the popular modern Scottish novelists – Stevenson, Munro, Compton Mackenzie, George Blake and Eric Linklater – but now I discovered the novelist who changed my whole way of thinking about the Scottish novel, Lewis Grassic Gibbon. It was *Sunset Song* that did it, but soon I was reading everything I could find by Gibbon and his other self, J. L. Mitchell. And then I was reading the prose works of C. M. Grieve and Hugh MacDiarmid and here, indeed, was another hero for a young man.

Soon I was no longer content with just borrowing the books from the public library and I began to look seriously for the works of Gibbon and MacDiarmid in second-hand bookshops which I had haunted ever since leaving school. The first book of poems that I bought by MacDiarmid was his *Selected Poems* edited by Crombie Saunders. Having really read only novelists, apart from anthology poetry at school which I had rejected, I did not know enough about poetry to be bowled over by MacDiarmid's poetry in this selection. At this time I was attracted to him as a rebel and nationalist rather than as a poet. I was all for the novel and thought poetry played out. But quite soon after finding the *Selected Poems* I was fortunate enough to get a second-hand copy of *A Drunk Man Looks at the Thistle* in Glen's shop in Parliamentary Road, Glasgow – it was the first edition and cost me five shillings. The man who ran Glen's kept books like that hidden away in the back shop and I had been pestering him for some time before he brought out anything by MacDiarmid. Not that there was any great demand for MacDiarmid at this time, as the price indicated. Another shop I kept visiting, opposite the Mitchell Library, had a most knowledgeable owner, but to him MacDiarmid was a socialist poet of the thirties whom he linked with Auden. Anyway, I had a copy of *A Drunk Man*. I was bowled over. Never had I thought that poetry like this existed; a poetry which spoke to me directly and yet was also beyond me in many places. A new world was opened up for me just as it had been (although to a lesser extent as I knew what the novel could do) when I first read *Sunset Song*.

I was lucky enough to get a copy of *Sangschaw* – also in Glen's and again for five shillings – and once more my whole concept of what poetry could do was changed. I do not remember having any difficulty with the Scots and took it just as part of the revelation I had experienced with regard to poetry. My notebook gives a checklist, compiled at this time, of the works of both Gibbon and MacDiarmid. The books by MacDiarmid that are ticked, indicating I owned them, are *Sangschaw, A Drunk Man, Selected Poems* (Saunders), *Contemporary Scottish Studies* and *Scottish Eccentrics*. But by this time I was reading everything by MacDiarmid that I could find in libraries. I had also discovered Sydney Goodsir Smith's poetry and in my notebook there is a checklist of works by him that I knew. The first list consisted only of *Under the Eildon Tree* but at a later date, judging by the change of ink, I added *So Late into the Night*.

When I travelled to Edinburgh to attend college part-time I used to buy the *Scottish Journal* at the bookstall in Kirkcaldy station. This was published and edited by William Maclellan, but for me it was dominated by the writings in verse and prose of Hugh MacDiarmid. Heady days for a young man. There was also, soon, the revived *Voice of Scotland*, edited by MacDiarmid of course. And then I was reading *Lines Review* and visiting Callum Macdonald, its publisher and printer, in his newsagent's and printing shop in Marchmont Road to get a copy of the Edinburgh University publication *Jabberwock* which he had printed. I wanted *Jabberwock* because it had included a radio talk by MacDiarmid as well as reproducing a photograph of the Benno Schotz head of MacDiarmid – that was in 1955. By then I was well and truly involved, as a reader, in the modern Scottish literary movement with its nationalistic supports. I never thought of getting to know any of the writers although I was still writing short stories and an attempted novel. By 1955 I was also quite well educated in the whole history of Scottish literature, having read a lot of the works and also the histories old and new, including *Scottish Poetry. A Critical Survey*, edited by James Kinsley, when it was published in 1955. The bibliography published in Sydney Goodsir Smith's *A Short Introduction to Scottish Literature* (1951) was very useful to me in my studies and the book itself was an excellent counterbalance to the books which see Scottish literature as an appendage to English literature. Goodsir Smith's book was written under the influence of MacDiarmid's advocacy of the 'Caledonian Antisyzygy'. By 1956, when I was a full-time student at Edinburgh College of Art, I was fully under the spell of MacDiarmid's poetry and theories of literature. I set some of his poetry in type in the Art College but pulled only a few proofs.

My first meeting with MacDiarmid was also whilst I was at the college. He came one evening to give a talk to what was only a handful of students. He had copies of the *Scottish Journal* with him and pulled them out of his old attaché case as he spoke. But for me the highlight of the evening was the long session of questions and discussion afterwards. I well believe we would still be there imposing on our generous speaker if the caretakers had not evicted us from the college at locking-up time. I went to that talk expecting to meet the firebrand of his prose works and, indeed, in his talk he was most forceful. In the question time, despite some very ignorant English imperialistic attitudes from an English questioner, the poet was very kind and gentle in his replies. This I was a little disappointed in, although I enjoyed the way he still effectively replied for all his kind politeness. I exchanged a few words with our speaker afterwards – in the gents' toilet in the basement of the building!

In May 1956 I started my National Service in the RAF and whilst home on leave that same year I picked up a copy of the first issue of the bibliographical magazine *The Bibliotheck* with Geoffrey Wagner's checklist of the writings of Lewis Grassic Gibbon. I was absolutely bowled over by this checklist which gave a lot of critical references in periodicals as well as Mitchell/Gibbon's books, etc. Within days I was in the Mitchell Library making tentative beginnings for a decent checklist of MacDiarmid's works. I spoke to the librarian there, Mr Hepburn, and he already had the beginnings of a list in card-index form which he showed me. *The Bibliotheck* was published from Glasgow University Library and I went to see the editor, but he was not available. Not that he would have encouraged a young amateur like myself, I imagine.

On 4th January 1957 my wife and I were married whilst I was on leave from the RAF. I have already quoted the last poem of 'Walkin in Fife' which describes us taking a short walk to meet the Reverend Davidson and as is perhaps to be expected, I have written a poem of our honeymoon. It is from 'Scotland's Hert' from *Realities Poems:*

III

MEMORIALS

We walk haund in haund frae Tarbert
back to Arrochar. Frae lochside to lochside.
Frae Lomond to Long. It's ten ablow
freezin and snaw on the grund. We hae
this tourist trap o summer to oursels. Only
our braiths hing in the January air
and we can stop alane
aneath a tree for a quick touch o lips. And find
we're aside the War Memorial.

But we are aff doun the road to Arrochar
haund in haund and the Cobbler* lookin doun
on us. And to us
a memorial to our honeymoon
set black and shairp agin the pure blue sky.
A memorial o luve as that ither to the few that
kent them
– as it is to us!

In July of that year we returned to Arrochar and an incident from that visit is described in the sequence 'Of Philosophers and Tinks' in *Realities Poems.* This sequence is of a gathering of friends in a pub, as I

*The mountain is also called Ben Arthur

used to do with male friends only when I was a dance hall haunter
before I met my wife, and although we solved the problems of the
world, spiced with much humour, none of us was a professional philosopher or a married man, as is John in 'Philosophers and Tinks'. But
John has something of me in him as I tended to act the 'intellectual' of
the group and, as in the poem, my friends were more than capable of
taking the mickey out of inflated seriousness. So I quote three verses
from the sequence to show the debunking and also, in the middle
section, a true scene from our holiday. But behind the debunking there
is also serious philosophical comment. Sections V and VII are friends
of John speaking to him whereas VI is John himself speaking to his
wife:

V

REVELATION

We ken God externally and in complete
essence in the mind, you say. But passions
are the obscurin mist atween us and Him, Spinoza
you say. I'd kent it was weakenin

but this is serious. It maun be aa
that whisperin o sweet naethings . . .

VI

BOARDIN HOUSE TEA

You walked upon the lush burn-side gress
and the joyfu cauld o heich spate
wi peat-broun watter and edges sae green.
And yet us paddlin and wagglin our taes in it.

A whisper breathin in your ear as the nou
and then my sock cairrit aff dounstream
frae the rocks. Twistin owre wee watterfaas
and swirlin slawly in deep still pools.

And us efter it leapin and hoppin by the side
and frae stane to stane. The ebb and flow
o the chase a flux and counterflux
and wi laughter that is wi us still here in this pub.

My breath comin quick as yours,
we race doun to the lochside house
and warmth on the rug by the fire
– and wunnerin what Mrs MacDonald thocht,

efterwards, as she served us our tea.

VII

AMBITIONS

I'm sayin to you wi Spinoza it'll be
an *intellectual* luve. A luve o God. A union
o thocht and emotion and gien true joy
kennin Truth for itsel. You're a famous luver

but you're no makin it wi God.

I was at the time of my marriage, and for the rest of my National Service, stationed at RAF Wyton, a few miles from Huntingdon, and my wife and I first lived in rented rooms in the very rural village of Houghton. But my wife was working as secretary to Marshall Sisson, the architect, and he and his wife offered us a flat they had created on the top floor of their large Georgian house in Godmanchester, another village near to Huntingdon. This house had been requisitioned during the 1939-45 war by the government and it was to it that the German atomic scientists were first taken at the end of the war in Europe. Mrs Sisson always felt they had left an eerie atmosphere behind them.

The Sissons were very kind to us and invited us to parties they gave and so I got to know how the English upper classes live. Mostly I did not approve of their politics but civilised and cultured people they mostly were – and no doubt still are. The Sissons are now both dead so the third last line of a verse from my poem 'Houses', which I have already quoted from, is not now true:

IV

There are people livin in my houses.
I walk unner chestnut trees and cross lawns
kept by a resident gairdner. I enter by a door
wi decorative fanlicht. The windaes are weill-proportioned.
There's a stane haa, corridors wi Regency colours
and chairs wi seat fabrics to match. An elegant
stair turns upwards. A vase stauns in an alcove.
The rooms dounstairs are large and civilised like the
first-floor bedrooms. A drawing-room wi period furniture
and a grand piano afore the windae. The fire-place
has a pile o logs at the side. The book room
has comfortable airmchairs and a desk wi typewriter.
I hae warked there and lived in some style. I dout
it's cheyned muckle being still in the same haunds.
The stair-carpet is deep and leads to our flet
and me a husband o that house.

More recently, in 1983, I have written of the Sisson's house, Farm Hall, in my sequence *The Stones of Time* and I will quote it later.

Whilst living in Godmanchester I attended Cambridge Art School part-time and my wife and I spent many Saturdays in Cambridge and got to know the city very well. I envied the undergraduates who lived in college and whilst I would not give up my past I do think the educational road of the public school/Oxbridge social group does give a cultural and a social unity which most Scots lack. But this lack of unity can be an asset rather than a handicap to a risk-taking writer. Not that I have a particularly high regard for the upper-class English when I meet them being loud-mouthed in the Highlands for the 'shootin' and fishin' '. But I did, and do, like Cambridge very much and wrote a poem about it in 'Traivellin Man':

IV

CAMBRIDGE

Thou hearest the Nightingale begin the Song of Spring
WILLIAM BLAKE

It's Spring. We micht expect to hear the nightingale,
being in Cambridge for the week. The daffodils are in bloom.
We've felt the pouer o brick and stane.
We've wandered in the Backs

by St John's and Trinity, Clare and King's
and heard the chimes o St Mary the Great
and the choir in full voice in michty King's.
Wha could forget the old court of Clare?

We hae browsed in David's bookshop and his stall,
read in the University Library, and looked at
the Titians, the Peter Brueghel and Rembrandt's
Man in a Plumed Hat in Fitzwilliam Museum.

We hae been out to Ely and seen the Cathedral
rise magnificently frae the fens
white agin the lang horizon o the black sile
– and lose naething at close quarters.

Bricks and stane rich as words
or chimes or voices in perfect harmony
but there's the flet, black fens pouerfu as
ony heich hill. And the daffodils in bloom.

In some ways, such as living out with my wife in very congenial surroundings, I was very lucky in my National Service, but the actual time involved with the service I hated. It was both a terribly boring time and yet a time of anxiety in that you never knew what they were going to do with you next. It felt to me that I had lost control of my own destiny. And what a waste of time. I have written, I think, only three poems on my actual RAF time. Perhaps the best of them is a nightmare section in *On Midsummer Evenin Merriest of Nichts?*:

> *National* Service!
> A sort of nichtmare
> nou near happy nostalgie
> – sometimes
> and sometimes no!
>
> Respond! Respond!
>
> Birlin thochts round and round
> carved in the deepest cave.
> Me. Me.
> Me, I ken, but auld as the rocks
> wi auldest pentin. And bell
> cracked and proclaimin Liberty
> but pushin me to answer
> its caa. It is time. It is
> time. Time to answer. Yes, sir.
> Yes, sir. Run, run
> be on time. And pintin finger
> frae braidit airm saying
> go, go, do, do. Accept. All will be
> well. Do as you are told! And ring
> ring of telephone awakenin frae the safety
> of sleep and voice to be answered.
> And een starin close in
> on and on focusin into
> me.
>
> Birlin thochts round and round
> flashin across ahint my een
> as, out of the nicht,
> saft fitsteps leave their mark. And spyin ee
> aye there through a keyhole a licht
> movin back through the wrang end of a telescope
> on and on deep into the surroundin daurk.
> Go. Go. Move. Move.
>
> My heid birls
> afore hypnotic lichts
> flashin and passin into a fallin daurkness.
>
> Respond! Respond!

And pintin finger frae braidit airm
and striped airm straucht by his side
and words spat out: 'Take him away!'

The pintin finger kens best.
Yes, sir. Run, run.

During my time at Godmanchester/Wyton I acquired a ticket for the
Reading Room of the British Museum and when I had the necessary
money I travelled up to London on Saturdays. This was the beginning
of a long period of total obsession with MacDiarmid's writings. By the
time I came out of the RAF in May 1958 I can say, looking back, that I
knew his writings very well and was completely under his influence. I
never thought to approach the great man himself. The complete
work – in all its vast extent in uncollected poems and essays – was
what I was after. By now I was writing up my own findings and during
my holiday following demob, which I theoretically spent with my wife
at her parents' home in Fife, I lived in the Edinburgh Public Library,
George IV Bridge, where I was greatly helped by Miss Catherine
Dickson.

I got a job as a typographic designer in London quite close to the
British Museum and from the Spring of 1958 to the early part of 1959 I
spent my lunch-breaks and many Saturdays in the Reading Room. In
Autumn 1958 came a blow to me – the publication of W. R. Aitken's
excellent checklist of the books and pamphlets of MacDiarmid in *The
Bibliotheck* – a professional had beaten me to the bibliographical side
so far as the books and pamphlets were concerned, but I was by now
well into writing a book, of which the bibliography was only a part.
Also I had researched the poetry and prose uncollected in books and
available only in magazines and newspapers. This periodical research
gave my work a lot of its strength and uniqueness. So I did not feel too
discouraged.

By early summer 1959 I had finished the first version of *Hugh
MacDiarmid and the Scottish Renaissance* but I kept finding new facts
and my wife had to type this massive work a second time, in 1960,
although she was pregnant. I let the book lie for some reason – being
perhaps too exhausted and too involved in a new job at Watford
College of Technology. At any rate it was not until early in 1962 that I
wrote to Hugh MacDiarmid, sending him the bibliography to my book
and asking him some questions. I received a very kind letter in reply,
but I decided that my own research was more accurate than Dr
Grieve's memory of exact dates and sequences of his life and work –
understandably enough. This led to my going to visit him at Brownsbank for the first time. I went by bus which arrived at lunchtime and as

this seemed an inconvenient time I explored the immediate area of Candymill village. Then I walked up that farm track for the first time and knocked on Brownsbank's door with its thistle knocker. MacDiarmid appeared at the door and it was obvious that although I was expected he had no idea who I was – I was not what he had expected; I think my youthfulness surprised him. I will never, of course, forget that first visit with the great man in his customary chair before the tall pigeon-holed unit which he told me came from a lawyer's office. I wrote a poem about him sitting before these pigeon holes, or grid, and it was eventually printed in *Poems Addressed to Hugh MacDiarmid* which I edited and published in 1967 for his seventy-fifth birthday. It was also absorbed into my long sequence 'In Memoriam Hugh MacDiarmid' which I wrote in 1983.

TO HUGH MACDIARMID
(AT BROWNSBANK)

Aside the bleezin fire I see you a movin heid
Afore a muckle daurk grid
Haudin fechtin petterns I glint within
Thae great lines
Risin frae your heid.

I see you a sma still haun lying in the shadows
O that aye movin heid
But fremit lookin wi it and aa
Thae great lines
Risin frae your heid.

But that fine still haun moves to your heid
And baith are ane
Afore the movin petterns hail in
Thae great lines
Risin frae your heid

I now began to correspond with MacDiarmid and another result of my visit was that he gave me permission to print and publish in pamphlet form forgotten or lost poems that I had found in my researches for my book.

I sent my synopsis of *Hugh MacDiarmid and the Scottish Renaissance* to two publishers who were not interested, but the third one – Chambers – asked to see it and, after long delays, it was published in November 1964, by which time we were living in Bishopbriggs, Glasgow. I shall always be grateful to T. C. Collocott, then Managing Director of Chambers, for taking on this book which started me on a literary career with something of a bang at a quite early age. The book was very widely reviewed and I do not remember an attacking or nasty one. Norman MacCaig was very kind in reviews in *The Listener* and *New Statesman*, writing in the latter: 'Duncan Glen has made a splendid job of what he meant to do. He is balanced, clear and immensely thorough. I could hardly fault him in terms of emphasis on this or that detail of the complicated scene and where I could the details were unimportant'. G. S. Fraser in *The Guardian* summed up his impression: 'The final impression one is left with is of a poetic personality that commands respect, and that proudly does not ask to be loved or liked'. Chambers gave a launching party for my book in the coffee room above the Edinburgh Bookshop in George Street. There were gathered many poets, artists and others of the modern Scottish cultural scene. MacDiarmid, who had been entertained all afternoon by American journalists, was at his most mischievous there and afterwards at dinner in the George Hotel, although he spoke most kindly at the party of my work – 'a labour of love' he called it – and my book.

Hugh MacDiarmid's cottage, Brownsbank, at Candymill as it was on October 25, 1968.
Photograph by Arthur Thompson.

CHAPTER 11

Stones of Time

DESPITE the basic insecurity for me of being a National Serviceman, my wife and I had many pleasant times in the flat lands of Huntingdonshire and also of Cambridgeshire and the cathedral city of Peterborough. That flat landscape has left a lasting impression on my mind although it did not feature markedly in my poetry until after we revisited it in the summer of 1983. In that fine summer we also visited other flat lands with fine buildings including Lincoln. Out of these visits of the summer of 1983 and my fifties memories of Huntingdonshire and Cambridgeshire and Peterborough came much of my sequence, *The Stones of Time*. But that sequence of poems is not only concerned with churches and cathedrals rising high to the sky but also with the bombers high in the sky and heavy with nuclear bombs. It is also concerned with things Scottish including Markinch and Edinburgh and with things personal including memories of my wife and myself together in Fife as well as Huntingdonshire. My poet friend Margaret Gillies is another thread, if I may so describe her, running through the sequence. But having written in the last chapter of our days in Huntingdonshire, I would quote here poems of flat lands of England. Although I only saw Lincoln Cathedral for the first time in the summer of 1983, as I write it is my favourite English building and Geoffrey of Lincoln, although known only through his constructions, the English architect I most admire. So I print here the whole of the Lincoln Cathedral section of *The Stones of Time* as well as poems on, to use the old names, Huntingdonshire, Cambridgeshire and Peterborough.

CATHEDRAL

Touch stone
and leap centuries.

Make journeys
into the past
and peer to know
the constructors.

Here all is vision
and tactile joy
crossing time.

Stand by open doors
tunnelling vision
through defused light
and rising stone.

We stand high
for a time
touching silence
loud
with the constructed past.

HORIZONS

Lean out of the railway carriage
window
and see the black fen soil
and the broad horizon
extending to eternity.

But look round
and the lantern tower
of Ely cathedral
rising in other sky
and other reality
beyond any horizon
measured
by man.

FLAT COUNTRY

Think of the villages
and flat lands of Huntingdonshire.
And the river Ouse broad and grey
spreading over the wide lands.

Lie by Ouse
and there seen
across its wide waters
the towers and spire of
Hemingfords.

There St Margaret
and St James
churches
from the thirteenth century.

Hemingford Abbots
and Hemingford Grey.

I think of the hurricane
of 1741.

A spire lowered
to truncated height
yet rising grandly still above
the broad river
and flat lands.

Lie again by Ouse
and see the towers
and the spire
of the Hemingfords.

But cross the river
and what of time
playing on
these speculative
1960's or 70's
bungalows?

SUPPORTS

I remember the supporting
misericords
of St Mary's Godmanchester
I peer again
at fox and goose
falcon
wyvern
cat
rabbit
dog
horse
lion
monkey
and the initials
of William Stevens
vicar in 1470-81.

Think of
five hundred years

and another two hundred
to touch the nameless mason
of materials
on the West Tower

high to the night sky . . .

WYTON

Think again of the flat lands
of Huntingdonshire.

The towers and spires
of country churches
going back in time.

Norman and thirteenth
century.
And the hurricane
of 1741
truncating spires
reaching to the sky.

Think of rural village Wyton.

But what of RAF Wyton
up the road
and V-bombers
taking off
into the sky
night and day.

Think again of the paired lancets
in the chancel
of St Margaret and All Saints
being early thirteenth century.

And over these flat lands
the wide open sky . . .

LINCOLN CATHEDRAL

I

I have forgotten the train journey
through flat, loamy Lincolnshire.
But outside the station
I remember over-well
the disappointment of the flat
shopping street
apeing a thousand others.

But then Steep Hill
civilised with cars banned
and central rail to help us up
by real-ale and real-food pub,
by tasteful art-galleries,
by well-bred antique dealers' displays,
by Good Food Guide restaurants.
A hill for civilised tourists
above this flat county.

But then the top.
Approach by mellow precincts
but there
suddenly
towers reaching to the sky
and wide-open door
tunnelling awed vision
through glowing light and rising stone,
through emotions and understandings
beyond any civilised Steep Hill,
highest savage Alpine peak
or any loamy language.

II

On the train I prepared myself
from learned book.
I know of Bishop Alexander
powerful
twelfth-century man.
I anticipated his portals
and decorative work.
His beasts,
affronted beasts,
birds,
grotesques,
naked couple,
snakes biting their vitals
and fighting eagles.

I think how he built
castles too
at Newark, Banbury
and Sleaford.

III

I know of the great St Hugh
becoming a bishop in 1186
only a year after
catastrophe to the Norman cathedral.
I know he started rebuilding
in 1192.

I know of later
masters of Lincoln
after his time. Of
Michael
and other Alexander

but over all
I search for contact
with the great constructor
of St Hugh. For some link with
Geoffrey de Noiers
master of architects.

IV

Here atop this hill
enter through these doors
and scholarly words gone
down Steep Hill.
Here joy and awe
in rising images.
I reach out
to the Single One
worshipped in this
creation of man.

V

But a place of people.
Enter a chapel
and there's a man praying.
Enter another
and there's a man peering close
at angel
or demon or prophet. He has
his camera at the ready
on tripod. Enter other space
and there's me
in my search for Geoffrey's
personality
out of the mediaeval night.

VI

But still I concentrate
and peer
into the unknowable past
to make contact with you
Geoffrey. I know
your creative mind and eye.
I touch stone
and am astride the bridge
between your co-ordinating, joyful mind
and mine.

VII

Geoffrey de Noiers of Lincoln
I see you bent over table
deep in creative thought
setting up your drawings
for your great work. Just my
indulgence. I know nothing personal
of you
'constructor'. And yet know all
that matters. Your work
leaping centuries. And
a chuckle behind the rising stone.

VIII

Geoffrey
your blank arcading
with round shafts. Your
polygonal shafts
with concave sides.
A unique mind
at serious play.

You innovatory to near excess
creating pattern,
space, syncopation
and vistas close-up
and afar. All success.
And known
in stone.

Lively stiff-leaf capitals,
deeply, richly moulded arches.
Your favourite detached shafts
giving us space
back and forward
as your syncopated arcading.

And. And. And
the Crazy Vault of Lincoln
out of your twisting
and unifying imagination.
You bent over creating. Your
imagination raising
the first purely decorative rib vault
with your heavy syncopation
so the historian tells us. But

I reach out alone
to your vision
in stone. A pattern of joy and glory
raising up ourselves
beyond self.

QUARRIES

Cross other flat lands.

Think of the brickworks
of Peterborough
and the town
being made new
as a development area
of the twentieth century.

But think of
Barnack stone
and mediaeval wood.

Think of the cathedral
and wooden ceilings.

Stand in the nave
and look up to ceiling of *c.* 1220
still with original colouring.

See the figures of
kings and queens,
saints,
a Janis head,
monster feeding on the bleeding
limbs of a man.
See architect with L-square
and dividers.
See monkey on a goat.

And eyes down
and along the leading
lifting
majesty
of the stone.

I think of the quarries
of Barnack
and men working there
eighteen centuries

or more . . .

FARM HALL

Think again
of the flat lands
of Huntingdonshire.

The Chinese bridge
of Godmanchester
to be crossed
to the islands of
the Ouse.

And walk along the banks.
A view across
to Farm Hall
finest house
of the village.

Be personal I say again.

There we lived
my young wife and young me.
There we lived
by generosity of Marshall Sisson,
architect,
and his wife
Marjorie.

Built in 1746
for Charles Clarke
Recorder of Huntingdon.
A grand house
yet
plain parallelpiped
with three storeys
of good red and rubbed brick.
To the front
five bays
with pedimented three-bay projection
and a parapet.

How can I forget the Tuscan porch
right onto the street,
or the genuine old railings.

How forget
the chestnut trees
in the garden
to the side.

How forget
the lime avenue
and, closer, the enclosed
rose garden.

And inside
how forget
the finely-detailed staircase
or the cross corridor
with elegant chairs.

Or the drawing room
with period furniture
and grand piano.
How forget book room
with rare editions
and fine desk
with typewriter.

I am told Farm Hall
has
a piano mobile
on the first floor
but in the Sisson's
time
there were bedrooms.

And we lived on the second
floor
looking down on
the chestnut trees.
And moving down to appraise
the English earl
and the lords and ladies
and county gentry
who gathered
for champagne and caviar.

And us the Scottish
outsiders
at these cultivated,
cultured parties.

Oh yes, aye, the civilisation
in that
the finest house
of Godmanchester.

How can I forget
the fine
marble chimney pieces.

How forget that German
atomic scientists
were taken there
in 1945.

They left an eerie
atmosphere
said Mrs Sisson.

And yet there still
the garden wall
with its gates
c. 1746.

Duncan Glen with the Grieves outside Brownsbank, October 25, 1968.

CHAPTER 12

A Small Press and Hugh Macdiarmid

THROUGHOUT his career as poet, essayist, critic, propagandist, and controversialist, Hugh MacDiarmid was associated with a quite considerable number of small presses or publishers. He was one himself – a small publisher, that is. His first book, *Annals of The Five Senses* (1923), was published by himself from Links Avenue, Montrose, and he published other books and magazines from there.[1] In the thirties, whilst in London MacDiarmid was a director of the Unicorn Press which published his own *First Hymn to Lenin and other poems* (1931). *Second Hymn to Lenin* was published separately by Valda Trevlyn, or Mrs C. M. Grieve, in 1932. MacDiarmid's early and major collections of poetry in Scots were published by the ultra-established firm of Blackwoods, of magazine and nineteenth-century publishing fame. It is eternally to their credit that they published these four early collections by Hugh MacDiarmid although they could perhaps have put more effort into actually selling them. All credit, however, to the gentleman at Blackwoods who had the judgement and courage to discover and publish MacDiarmid in the twenties – *Sangschaw* (1925), *Penny Wheep* (1926), *A Drunk Man Looks at the Thistle* (1926) and *To Circumjack Cencrastus* (1930). Victor Gollancz, who published *Stony Limits and other poems* in 1934, showed equal courage as by the middle thirties MacDiarmid had moved into the freer and more political forms of his middle period; the period when he wrote such major poems as 'On a Raised Beach', 'Lament for the Great Music' and 'Stony Limits'. Macmillans – and I believe it was the future Prime Minister himself – included MacDiarmid in their Contemporary Poets series where he now looks surprisingly out of place among such poets as Elizabeth Belloc, Yvonne French, E. H. W. Meyerstein and G. H. Vallins. It is true that Patrick Kavanagh is also represented in the series but MacDiarmid now stands out as an exceptional choice. Until the publication of his *Collected Poems* by the Macmillan Company of New York in 1962 that was the last time MacDiarmid's poetry was to be published by a major publisher, although prose works were published by Jarrolds, Routledge, Batsford, and by Methuen who published his first autobiographical volume, *Lucky Poet* (1943).

[1] See Duncan Glen. *Hugh MacDiarmid and the Scottish Renaissance*, p. 100. See also bibliography of MacDiarmid's works, pp. 245-262.

In the twenties the Porpoise Press of Edinburgh was doing a notable job as a small native encourager of Scottish literature by making available both Scottish classics of the past and the works of contemporary writers. They encouraged novelists such as Neil Gunn and George Blake, and their poetry broadsheets were an excellent series even if, as is inevitable, most of the poets are now names known only to specialists in the history of modern Scottish literature. Still, MacDiarmid's *Lucky Bag* (Porpoise Press Broadsheet 4, third series) shows that they could also pick a winner although by 1927 they were really backing someone else's fancy in the literary stakes. Eneas Mackay, that fine and courageous printer-publisher from Stirling, showed more courage when he printed MacDiarmid's *Scots Unbound and other poems* in 1932 as by then the poet had indeed unbound the Scots muse and the Scots language from the long-established ways of the post-Burnsian versifiers. This was a book to make him the prophet of the new younger Scots makars, as of course was *A Drunk Man Looks at the Thistle* – and indeed as were the short lyrics of *Sangschaw* and *Penny Wheep*.

After the 1939-45 war the small printer-publishers with whom MacDiarmid was most closely associated were the Caledonian Press and William Maclellan, both of Glasgow. It was the Caledonian Press which published the second edition of *A Drunk Man Looks at the Thistle* in 1953. That this masterpiece, and perhaps the greatest poem in the whole range of Scottish poetry, was so long out of print is a disgrace to Scottish and to British publishing. The Caledonian Press published a creditable number of pamphlet poems by MacDiarmid and also printed his quarterly magazine *The Voice of Scotland*. The press was run by Callum Campbell and his brother Kenneth and although it went the way of most publishing presses and soon ceased to exist, the two brothers were not finished yet. In the fifties they founded the printing firm of Castle Wynd Printers just off the Castle Esplanade in Edinburgh and it was under that imprint that the third edition of *A Drunk Man* appeared in 1956. They also reissued *Stony Limits* and the title poem of *Scots Unbound* as *Stony Limits and Scots Unbound* in 1956; and more than reissued in that poems were included in that book which had been excluded for legal reasons from the first edition of *Stony Limits* – poems such as the wondrous 'Harry Semen' and the long 'Ode to all Rebels' which still awaits a sympathetic critic. The Castle Wynd imprint also made available *Three Hymns to Lenin* (1957), *The Battle Continues* (1957), and the prose works *Burns Today and Tomorrow* (1959). Also promised as 'forthcoming' were *Sangschaw* and *Penny Wheep* but Castle Wynd Printers Limited were absorbed into another firm before that was achieved. An issue of *The*

Voice of Scotland which was then at galley proof stage also failed to appear because of this merger.

Modern Scottish poetry also owes a major debt to William Maclellan, originally Hope Street, Glasgow, whose publishing activities helped to give us the second wave of the Scottish Literary Renaissance in the forties. He published MacDiarmid's *In Memoriam James Joyce* (1955). He also published the 'Poetry Scotland' series of poetry collections which included two by Hugh MacDiarmid: *Selected Poems* edited by R. Crombie Saunders (1944) and *A Kist of Whistles* (1947). This series, with the annual anthology *Poetry Scotland* edited by Maurice Lindsay, was a fine encouragement to Scottish poetry in the forties.

Another publisher who has greatly encouraged Scottish poetry is Callum Macdonald of Edinburgh. Starting as a small printer turned publisher in the basement of his newsagent's shop in Marchmont Road, Callum Macdonald has made an important contribution to modern Scottish literature. MacDiarmid was not closely associated with Macdonald but his essay on Francis George Scott was published under that imprint as a tribute to the composer on his seventy-fifth birthday. Callum Macdonald's greatest contribution to Scottish poetry has been in publishing the works of Robert Garioch and Sydney Goodsir Smith and the magazine *Lines Review*. However it was Serif Books, another small printer-publisher, who first published Smith's *Under the Eildon Tree* in 1948.

With the possible exception of Eneas Mackay's publication *Scots Unbound* (which is good only by comparison with the others) none of these books by MacDiarmid published by small presses could be considered fine typography. William Maclellan did try to produce *In Memoriam James Joyce* as a fine book but the press work is uneven from not-very-good Linotype slugs. The illustrations by R. D. Fergusson are interesting but not really an integral part of the book, as is so often the case when a painter turns illustrator. The paper is Basingwerk and the cloth binding of reasonable trade quality. There was also a special issue bound in leather, signed by the author and the artist. A very important book and a well-intentioned piece of book design but not an outstanding example of fine printing. Of the typographic quality of *The Kind of Poetry I Want* (1961), published by K. D. Duval, there can, however, be no doubt. It was designed, printed and bound by that master of fine printing, Giovanni Mardersteig of Verona. Since then Kulgin Duval has published, in conjunction with his partner Colin H. Hamilton, another two books by MacDiarmid which are Mardersteig, father and then son, designs and productions. They are an edition of *A Drunk Man Looks at the Thistle* with eight woodcuts by Frans Masereel, and *Direadh I, II and III*. These are very fine books indeed.

It was in 1958, whilst compiling the bibliography for my *Hugh MacDiarmid and the Scottish Renaissance*, that I first saw the poem 'Poetry Like the Hawthorn' which in August 1962 was to be planned as the first publication to appear under my 'imprint'. I found the poem in the magazine *Wales*; it had been incorporated into MacDiarmid's long poem *In Memoriam James Joyce* although at that time I did not associate it with that poem and thought I had made an important 'find'.

In 1958 the thought of a fine printing of the poem was only the indulgent fancy of a twenty-five years old professional typographic designer with a passionate enthusiasm for the work of Hugh MacDiarmid, but after I met Christopher Grieve at his home in July 1962 he wrote to me in August, with his usual generosity, 'of course I'll be very happy if you print "Poetry Like the Hawthorn" as you suggest'. I was more than happy and the type – 'Monotype' Bembo Italic for the poem – was hand-set and hand-printed by me. Although a professional designer of books, I had then no experience of the marketing side of publishing and madly under-priced the ordinary copies at 3s 6d and the special twenty-five signed copies at 10s 6d. The author generously wrote to his publisher, 'an elegant job, beautifully printed and produced'.

Poetry Like the Hawthorn was the start but not the first book I published. That was my own very short *Hugh MacDiarmid: Rebel Poet and Prophet* published as a tribute to both aspects of his character on his seventieth birthday – 11th August 1962 – under the imprint 'The Drumalban Press'.

One of the fruits of my research into the work of MacDiarmid was the discovery that his first Scots poems had appeared in an article he wrote for a small weekly paper *The Dunfermline Press* as poems written by a 'friend'. I can now, many years later, very clearly remember the excitement I felt when – in the Colindale newspaper library of the British Museum – I turned the pages of that paper to find these two Scots poems. Recognition of them as by MacDiarmid was instant as one of them was the famous 'The Watergaw'; the other was quite unknown and entitled 'The Blaward and the Skelly'. This poem is of no importance except as one of the first Scots poems MacDiarmid wrote, although the article is important as giving insight into how he first came to write in Scots. I consider finding this article one of the most important results of my researches, drawing attention as it does to Sir James Wilson's *Lowland Scotch as Spoken in the Lower Strathearn District of Perthshire* and the use of this book by MacDiarmid to write his first poems in Scots. In September 1962, for rather sentimental reasons, I set 'The Blaward and the Skelly' in type and printed ten copies on brown kraft paper.

My part-time publishing thoughts (printing thoughts really) now turned to small-leaflet publication of Scottish poets. Naturally I wished the greatest of them to be the first in the series. I designed the leaflets and had specimens set but the Macmillan Company of New York, to their eternal credit, had sensibly brought out MacDiarmid's *Collected Poems* and my plans fell through. I had, however, discovered in my MacDiarmid researches, as I have said, poems which I thought important but which had not been reprinted since their appearance in magazines in the thirties and forties. I suggested to Dr Grieve that I would like to publish some of these in limited editions. The first appeared in 1964 printed at my Drumalban Press which now had a Scottish address (my parents') with my planned return to the West of Scotland from Hemel Hempstead where we lived whilst I was lecturing in typographic design at Watford College of Technology. I was very pleased with a 'kinetic' title page with the words 'two poems' printed on a narrow black sheet and the turn-over to read as a continuation of the title *The Terrible Crystal: A Vision of Scotland* by Hugh MacDiarmid. My name and address were printed at the foot of the title page but not only, apparently, did no-one understand (understandably) my 'kinetic' title page but I got letters addressed to Hugh MacDiarmid at, or in, 'Duncan Glen', Skelmorlie, Ayrshire, and indeed for some years such an address was listed in *British Books in Print*. These letters came from buyers in America, England and even Scotland! There being an edition of only fifty-five copies, most letters arrived too late. A second leaflet-edition was printed but this was also limited to fifty copies or so as it was restricted to paper left over from the first printing.

Still continuing with collecting uncollected poems by MacDiarmid, I now put together a light-hearted collection of vituperative poems printed on thin board but, on showing it to Dr and Mrs Grieve, one of the poems was identified as being not by MacDiarmid. The periodical printing had misled me. These topical poems were of some interest I thought and eventually I used most of them – and others – in a small collection entitled *Poet at Play and other poems* which I privately printed in January 1965 as a surprise tribute to the poet and his 'friends', A. K. Laidlaw, Isobel Guthrie, James MacLaren, and Arthur Leslie, to whom the collection was dedicated. These 'friends' of Hugh MacDiarmid and Christopher Grieve had previously been introduced and discussed in my pamphlet *The Literary Masks of Hugh MacDiarmid*. 'Arthur Leslie' is an interesting character since Christopher Grieve used him in the early fifties to defend and explain himself against and to his Scottish enemies. I was very pleased to be able to include the 'Leslie' essay 'The Poetry and Politics of Hugh

MacDiarmid' as the first essay in *Selected Essays of Hugh MacDiarmid* which I edited and which was published by Cape in November 1969. As MacDiarmid on MacDiarmid this 'Leslie' essay is 'a uniquely appropriate introduction' to *Selected Essays*. *The Times Literary Supplement* (27th November 1969) saw the essay as a first one which 'signposts the reader very helpfully' into the other essays and as 'one of the best sustained expository pieces that MacDiarmid has written'. This essay, as I also said in my introduction to *Selected Essays*, 'was a reply to the abuse, neglect and misrepresentation that MacDiarmid suffered in the thirties, forties and fifties; it was a reply to the anti-cultural and anti-poetic and anti-Scottish forces which flourish in the Scottish climate'. The *TLS* reviewer (who was G. S. Fraser) saw *Selected Essays* as a collection which is able 'to give us a sense of the unity of MacDiarmid's mind; and to give us a sense that however parochial and cantankerous that mind may seem, in its listing of minor Scottish worthies and in its clinging to small feuds, it is a mind that has grappled, through a long life, with what are still living issues'.

To me, MacDiarmid's mind has been the most influential Scottish one of modern times and I have expressed my admiration for him often enough, sometimes in verse. I have already quoted one of my poems addressed to MacDiarmid but, according to critics of my work, one of the best poems I have written addressed to him would seem to be the following eight-liner:

THE NEW SCOTLAND
(for Hugh MacDiarmid)

Dear Christopher Grieve
like you I am returnin to Glasgow
efter long exile

I found you singin like a lintie
in the street
and doun the road in the park
they are lockin up the swings
for Sunday

The first six pamphlets which I published were printed by me on a sophisticated proofing press which I had access to while living in Hemel Hempstead and working in Watford, but when I returned to Glasgow in 1963 as editor for an educational publishing company I lost access to this printing machine and had to think of a way of .continuing my printing/publishing activities.

I bought a small machine really designed for printing cards and letterheadings – an 'Adana' platen – and type which filled two cases – 10pt and 12pt Baskerville – as well as a few leads and a very small quantity of imposing furniture. It was all that I could afford. The Adana machine cost £27 17/- including carriage, and the type etc. about £10. The only other outlay I had was printing ink and paper for the text and covers of each publication. I can claim to have started on about £40 in 1963 values.

My essay *The Literary Masks of Hugh MacDiarmid* was my first printing on the Adana. It had a sheet size which overlapped the edges of the machine as I printed a page at a time. The portrait illustrations of MacDiarmid I hand-drew onto the printed sheets. I had a master drawing placed against a window so that I could see to trace off onto the sheets.

I next printed MacDiarmid's *The Ministry of Water* which contained two poems, 'Prayer for a Second Flood' and 'Larking Dallier'. This pamphlet had an even larger paper size and really extended the little press to its limits. Often I had too little type to set up the complete text of these pamphlets and set a page or two, printed them, distributed the type back into the case, set the next pages, printed and so on. The printing was done with me kneeling before the little machine on the floor of our dining room. The type was set with the case on my knee in the living-room.

Another MacDiarmid pamphlet which came off my printing press was *The Fire of the Spirit*. The Scots poem 'By Wauchopeside' in this pamphlet was to me one of the pleasurable and memorable finds of my youthfully enjoyable but still head-splitting labours on a MacDiarmid bibliography. 'Diamond Body,' which goes with it, is another of these finds I remember so well. But 'By Wauchopeside' is my favourite of the poems by MacDiarmid that I rediscovered and printed. Who cannot fail to find joy and pleasure from its opening lines, and indeed from the whole poem, although I will restrict myself to quoting the first two verses:

> Thrawn water? Aye, owre thrawn to be aye thrawn!
> I ha'e my wagtails like the Wauchope tae,
> Birds fu' o' fechtin' spirit, and o' fun,
> That whiles jig in the air in lichtsome play
> Like glass-ba's on a fountain, syne stand still
> Save for a quiver, shoot up an inch or twa, fa' back
> Like a swarm o' winter-gnats, or are tost aside,
>   By their inclination's kittle loup,
>   To balance efter hauf a coup.
>
> There's mair in birds than men ha'e faddomed yet.
> Tho' maist churn oot the stock sangs o' their kind

There's aiblins genius here and there; and aince
'Mang whitebeams, hollies, siller birks –
            The trees o' licht – I mind

I used to hear a blackie mony a nicht
Singin' awa' t'an unconscionable 'oor
Wi' nocht but the water keepin't company
(Or nocht that ony human ear could hear)
– And wondered if the blackie heard it either
Or cared whether it was singin' tae or no'!
O there's nae sayin' what my verses awn
To memories like these. Ha'e I come back
To find oot? Or to borrow mair? Or see
Their helpless puirness to what gar'd them be?
            Late sang the blackie but it stopt at last.
            The river still ga'ed singin' past.

W. R. Aitken has kindly written of these pamphlets of poems by
MacDiarmid which I published in the sixties: 'They must not be
dismissed as though they were irresponsibly conceived bibliographical
curiosities, produced in deliberately limited editions more for the glory
of the printer and publisher than for the poet. It is, for example, very
doubtful if the poems contained in *A Lap of Honour* (1967), the first of
the collections designed to supplement the *Collected Poems* of 1962,
and perhaps the best-planned recent volume of his poetry, would be
known but for Duncan Glen's succession of pamphlets, privately
printed between 1962 and 1967. Hugh MacDiarmid acknowledges that
"Duncan Glen . . . has done a great deal . . . to recover many poems I'd
lost sight of and forgotten I'd written".'

CHAPTER 13

Esk, Ewes and Wauchope

I HAVE referred to 'By Wauchopeside' as being my favourite amongst the poems by MacDiarmid that I rediscovered and printed. Recently Ruth McQuillan described the second poem of my sequence 'In Memoriam Hugh MacDiarmid' as follows: 'This, I'm sure, is the best poem of yours I've ever seen'. As an In Memoriam poem written in 1983 it is, of course, sad that MacDiarmid could not read this poem as I like to think he would have approved of the way I see some of our fellow countrymen and also pleased to see the references to Wauchope and other Langholm rivers that were so important to him in childhood and which are now immortalised in his poetry. I quote the whole of section two of 'In Memoriam Hugh MacDiarmid'.

II

In Crowdieknowe graveyaird I see you walkin alane
Movin amang your forebears' heidstanes slantit wi age.
    I'm the ane alane talkin, talkin to mysel, hopefully in sage
    Words tryin to mak personal rhymes and mebbe refrain again
        Agin fatefu, separatin daith.
    Like you I hae nae faitherly God for faith
    But there's thocht and memory baith
    Wi leid to staun obliquely in memory of you,
As lucky poet strivin for what is honest, heich and true.

I see the grison[1] movin doun the Canongate
Circumambulatin obstacle efter obstacle against the grain.
    Pourin round them like a train
    Come up against cornered folk. There's sleekit hate
        Frae auld against the young.
    Jim thinks on the girl to be won
    As black-suitit gents staun dourly agin aa fun,
    The grison could be seen as slitherin snake to tempt very soon
To sang and joy e'en thae daurk-mindit folk lang thocht immune.

I see vennel become daurk cave by Saramaca river.[2]
A torch shines on circle of land-crabs drappin tall periscope een
    To wave their huge pincers. Nou some seen

---

[1] A kind of weasel found in the Caribbean.
[2] Again Caribbean as are the other rivers mentioned.

Blawin bubbles that hiss, squeak and quiver
In the silence of the cave.
I turn my een up ither vennel and wave
To Auld Toun's May and Dave
There bricht wi fun and joy agin the daurkest nicht.
Will they succeed? Will they sing of life and licht?

I see the three-fingered sloth wi sub-human face
less absurd than three blunt paws, stumpy and insensitive.
By the banks of river Parva they live.
But what of them by Forth that pace and race
Up rat-race ladder to sub-normal tune?
Grey muggers are aa about the daurk toun
As cauld haar sweeps in frae the Forth dullin aa soun.
But there's licht in upstairs windae and ten fingers
Raised to accompany brave new choir of singers.

What of the pigmy ant-eater by Surinam river wha's een
On capture quickly fill to owre-flowin wi touchin tears?
Sentimentalists beware o haein nae fears,
Beware of the hidden armament soon seen
– Claws dense, tough and shairp as a gaff.
To walk by Saramaca, Surinam and Parva is nae laugh
But I ken Forth (or Clyde) and upricht men wha aye laugh
Seik or weill, drunk or sober, singin or cryin. They
face the false tears and strikin claws mony and mony a day.

I saw the grison doun the Canongate.
I see the land-crabs and sloth wi three fingers.
I see pygmy ant-eaters. But still I hear singers
Facin the fremit fauna. I hear, as it grew sae late,
The lilt of Border rivers. I hope,
And think of the licht frae clearest Wauchope.
Here nae need to shine torch or grope
In the daurk. Here's watters bricht wi licht
And of them we can aa hae a sicht.

But still the reflections frae Saramaca, Surinam and Parva rivers.
I see the Canongate bricht wi tropical licht.
For sure it's a fremit sicht
Revealin the true fauna by the northern rivers.
Wheesht, wheesht, douce street.
I sicht them that will sob and greet
Expectin a land that is southern sweet.
But licht shines and sangs are in the air
For them wi the ear to hear and the hairt to dare.

I hae walked, movin doun the ambulatory Canongate
Appraisin, lucky poet, sicht efter sicht against your standards.
Passin them round and round my harns as ither true bards.

But your daith is deep in my heid. It's late.
Wheesht, wheesht, city nicht.
I would hae true Border licht
As at last I face daith's micht
As infinite, eternal; but faith and hope
Live on frae lilt of singin Esk, Ewes and Wauchope.

Duncan Glen and Hugh MacDiarmid recording a conversation at Brownsbank in October 1968.
Photograph by Arthur Thompson.

CHAPTER 14

Akros Magazine and Akros Publications

EARLY IN 1965 I decided to edit a new Scottish poetry magazine and to attempt to set the type and to print it myself. There was at this time no Scottish poetry magazine appearing regularly except for the Gaelic magazine *Gairm*. The excellent *Lines Review* was appearing most irregularly at that time. Someone who encouraged me a lot was a young man I then worked with – Willie Macdonald. After much debate I decided to name the new magazine *Akros*. I found this name in an old edition of Chambers' *Twentieth-Century Dictionary*. The name is from the Greek root meaning 'highest and furthest out', as in Acropolis. I also chose the name for the suggestion of cutting across cliques and not least for the look of the word which I could see with my typographer's eye as a fine logotype. Willie Macdonald tells me that I pasted up the *Akros* logotype several times before I was satisfied with it – and even then I got it wrong as there is too much space between two of the letters, 'r' and 'o', although this was eventually corrected. Still, apart from that the logotype was all that remained constant in the design of the magazine throughout its life.

Encouraged by my young friend and colleague, and by the success in review terms of my book *Hugh MacDiarmid and the Scottish Renaissance*, I wrote to a number of known poets asking for poems. They all co-operated, including Norman MacCaig, Robert Garioch and J. K. Annand. I also wrote to Alastair Mackie whose work I had seen in a student magazine, although Alastair was no student but a teacher in Anstruther, Fife. Roderick Watson and James Rankin, who were students and whose work I had seen in a small student pamphlet, were others from whom I solicited poems. I have to take some pride in recognising the worth of these three poets at that time. I also had work from two English poets – Tony Connor and Jeremy Robson – and from Douglas Hill, a Canadian living in London. I forget how I made contact with Douglas Hill but I do remember that he helped a lot after *Akros* was printed by taking it round the London bookshops. Alan Bold, then just beginning to attract attention as a student poet and editor and critic was also in No. 1 as was Hugh Rae whom I had met when he worked in Smith's Glasgow bookshop and whose very successful first novel *Skinner* was about to be published.

Another contributor to No. 1 was Hugh MacDiarmid who gave me permission to reprint his rather forgotten poem 'The Burning Passion' but the poem in No. 1 which has become truly famous is Robert Garioch's 'At Robert Fergusson's Grave' which reads:

AT ROBERT FERGUSSON'S GRAVE
October 1962

Canongait kirkyaird in the failing year
is auld and grey, the wee roseirs are bare,
five gulls leam white agin the dirty air:
why are they here? There's naething for them here.

Why are we here oursels? We gaither near
the grave. Fergusons mainly, quite a fair
turn-out, respectfu, ill at ease, we stare
at daith – there's an address – I canna hear.

Aweill, we staund bareheidit in the haar
murnin a man that gaed back til the pool
twa-hunner year afore our time. The glaur

that haps his banes glowres back. Strang, present dool
ruggs at my hairt. Lichtlie this gin ye daur:
here Robert Burns knelt and kissed the mool.

So the first number of *Akros* appeared in August 1965 and it appeared thereafter at very regular intervals three times a year until October 1982 when it became an annual publication. But only one issue appeared annually as I found myself doing very little less work with an annual apart from the chores of despatching being reduced to once a year instead of thrice. I also found the long gaps between issues did not suit my temperament as an editor; I had to turn away too much good poetry and too many good new poets to whom I could have given the encouragement of publication when *Akros* appeared three times a year. So *Akros* came to an end with No. 51 in October 1983.

Eighteen years is a long time to edit a magazine and although I got a lot of pleasure from my work for *Akros*, I was glad, as was my wife, to call a halt. My last editorial prose words in *Akros* were: 'Without the support of my wife none of it would have been possible' and no more sincere words have ever been written.

On the day my wife took the last issue to the Post Office I prepared a little booklet for her with a poem for her which I wrote that day, and graphics from issues of *Akros*. One of the pieces of graphics was of a man walking out from between large quotation marks; under it I wrote, to my wife's pleasure and amusement, 'On his way – free'. Certainly I was glad to be free of rejecting hundreds and hundreds of poems and both of us were glad to be free of the chores of addressing many hundreds of envelopes three times a year as it was for seventeen years, and invoicing booksellers and making up dozens of parcels, and filling in scores of forms for subscription agents and doing the accounts year after year and so on and on. And me chasing up critics and reviewers who were bad at meeting deadlines which always hung over us. But not once in eighteen years did *Akros* appear late and of that we are both proud. So we were glad to be free but, of course, also sad after all the joy of the work and the pleasures of critical recognition and the joy of letters from many kind correspondents over the years from all over the world. The flood of mail after we sent out the last issue was most heartening and came from unexpected people. One correspondent kindly said that the end of *Akros* was the end of a literary epoch and another said it 'never became predictable' and was 'irreplaceable' because, he wrote, 'the personality of the editor made it unique'. The same writer said that *Akros* 'seemed to get better and better' which is a good thing to have said at the end although the early numbers give me personally much pleasure as I look back on them. It pleases me of course to look back through the whole long life of *Akros*.

The first issue is a very slim production and its actual press work is not good. Indeed, it is rather bad but then no small machine is made to cope with the quantity of type even of the single pages that I printed at a time. As with the MacDiarmid pamphlets, I had to set and print and distribute and set and so on. I seem to remember that I sent proofs to the contributors to No. 1 but after that I had no time to spend on such niceties.

I ran off (if my hand-printing can be so described) a separate pamphlet printing of MacDiarmid's 'The Burning Passion' which, as I have said, appeared in *Akros* 1. I liked to use type to the maximum once I had it set up. This was the last piece of printing I did in Bishopbriggs, Glasgow, as in September I started a new job in Preston, Lancashire, as a lecturer in graphic design at what was then the Harris College but is now Preston Polytechnic.[1] This move meant a decision had to be made on whether or not to continue printing and publishing the newly founded *Akros* magazine from an English address, but I never really had any doubts that it should continue. Soon we moved into our new home at 14 Parklands Avenue, Penwortham, Preston, and before long I was sitting in our new living-room setting the type for *Akros* 2 and printing it upstairs in a large spare bedroom we had but which was really my printing room. We had acquired from my father-in-law a large roll-top desk and the Adana machine sat on it. The desk

[1] Recently retitled Lancashire Polytechnic.

soon became stained with black printing ink and I had to keep the roll-top down when my father-in-law visited us so that he could not see how I had maltreated his fine old oak desk.

My father-in-law, Stephen Eadie, now dead, was a very fine and interesting man. When I first knew him he was station-master at Markinch which was an important station in freight terms due to Haig's, the whisky people, and Tullis Russell, the paper manufacturers, being in Markinch.

In a way Stephen Eadie reminded me of my maternal grandfather, George Tennent, in that both were great talkers or conversationalists and were surrounded by a large family, although my grandfather had more non-family visitors to his home than did my father-in-law. I have described some of the visitors to my grandfather's house in my sequence 'On a Fit-stool':

VII

NANE THE WAUR

It was kent as a guid mait house. Here
plump goose is no confined to ony special season.
And chickens soon haein their necks raxed
wi a jerk o the elbuck and plucked by willin
haunds. A haill pig in cauld-box
and delicacies pit aside for kent preferences.
And hams smoked and hung. And
new-baked scones and pancakes straucht frae girdle.
And the sponges and cakes o high-tea that
gars your teeth watter.

Aa wi feet unner the round table in the kitchen.
J. Lauchlin Watt the lawyer frae Hamilton,
Tom Grant the vet frae Cathkin Road End
and the Reverend Stoddart frae Ruglen. The weill-kent
faces o sociable neibours and mony anither
drappt in frae toun or village. And the dochters there
aside the sons, and mait and talk no the only
attraction o the house. And grandmither sat at last
and grandfaither in the centre as aye
wi his muckle chair moved round frae the fire
and kep on his knee. Aa the joy
o talk and lauchter
and freedom preached
in love and life. And aa the warld
so to be creatit.

Aa taen for themsels and to be themsels.
There's but ae rule. Aa flows but drink.

'Naebody leaves Daisybank waur
than they cam.'

   It may seem strange for so sociable a man to be tee-total but there
had been drinking problems amongst his older brothers and he had
taken the lesson. But to revert to my father-in-law, his most interesting
and most sociable days were probably when he was station-master and
harbour-master at the fishing village of Mallaig in the far north-west of
Scotland. There he was a real personage with the railway company, a
power in the land. My wife was born there and in 'A Sort of Renewal'
in *Realities Poems* I wrote a poem of her birth:

II

SEEVEN P.M.

It is seeven o'clock
and Christmas is but three days past.
I am soon to be fowre,
an eternity by your life time.
It is seeven o'clock in the hielants
and by the sea and you are cryin
in the daurk. The gulls are skreichin
owre the wee boats in the herbour
heavy wi fish. And a train steams
whistlin out o the station
for the touns o the south.
In that lallans south I am daein
what is nou forgotten or unplaceable.
But it is seeven o'clock
and I would like to be there
in the hielants by the sea and by the railwey
whaur you, forty the day,
were being born
at seeven o'clock in the evenin.

   But to get back to my father-in-law's desk and my using it as a base
for my printing machine. Another of Hugh MacDiarmid's then forgotten poems that I had discovered whilst researching *Hugh MacDiarmid
and the Scottish Renaissance* was 'Whuchulls' and this was printed in
Akros 3 and also as a pamphlet. For this separate printing of
'Whuchulls' I added some illustrations which I did by direct printing
from leaves and cut-up pieces of string for a portrait of MacDiarmid
which I superimposed on leaves for one of the illustrations. I got the
varied colour effects by hand-inking in two colours and the impression
was obtained by running a clean roller over the laid-on paper. It all

took hours and hours and for *Whuchulls* I had only cheap paper which was left over from *Akros* 3 – a false economy which I have not repeated. My own long poem 'Idols' which appeared in *Akros* 5, June 1967, was also reprinted as a pamphlet with decorations by me using several colours and employing printer's rules sometimes printed, and over-printed, at an angle to give optical effects. The poem was printed under my pseudonym of 'Ronald Eadie Munro' but the decorations were by Duncan Glen. The pseudonym was revealed in 1969 when Caithness Books published my collection of poems, *Kythings*, but it was a well-kept secret when my first pamphlet of poems, *Stanes*, was printed and published by the author in September 1966 from the Kinglassie, Fife, address to which my wife's parents had retired from Markinch, although the whole pamphlet was in fact set and printed by me in Penwortham just after I had printed *Akros* 3 and *Whuchulls*. I used good quality Basingwerk Parchment paper from Abbey Mills for *Stanes* and the Adana did a good job for me once again; I doubt if many people would guess that such a large page (size $9^5/8 \times 7^3/8$ in.) had been printed on such a small machine. *Stanes* included a frontispiece by me and this again was not printed from blocks but from a mixture of string and layers of cut-up card which was hand-inked. On this occasion the type was used for one publication only.

By the time I came to print *Akros* 4, issued in January 1967, our much-used Baskerville type was beginning to wear and I was also wearying of the labour of hand-setting, hand-distributing the type back into the case, and hand-printing, and for the first time I turned to commercial printing for the magazine in that twelve of the twenty-four pages of No. 4 were set and printed by Brian Lloyd whom I had met when he was a lecturer at what is now Preston Polytechnic and who also owned a small printing business, Lloyds of Blackburn. From that small job for No. 4 Brian Lloyd went on to print most issues of the magazine and he has been very patient in following my fussy demands as a magazine designer and, indeed, as a book designer as he has also printed many books and pamphlets for Akros Publications. Our relationship has been a very happy one and I know Brian treated *Akros* and Akros Publications books and pamphlets as work to which he gave special personal attention and in which he took real pride. I could not have found a more willing and enthusiastic printer for my publications.

The insert for *Akros* 4 was not the first job Brian Lloyd printed for me. The first was a pamphlet of poems by Giles Gordon entitled *Two and Two Make One* which was published in October 1966. This was the second in a series entitled 'Akros Poets', Alastair Mackie's *Soundings* having been the first. Alastair came to spend a weekend with us at Bishopbriggs just after *Akros* 1 had appeared and that weekend we planned *Soundings*, his first collection of poems. It is also the first publication with the imprint of Akros Publications; MacDiarmid's *The Burning Passion* was published as by the Akros Press. I hand-set and hand-printed *Soundings* in Penwortham with the sheets of paper laid out to dry all over the bed in the room which I have already described.

Soundings was launched with the following announcement in an advertising circular which I issued – and printed: 'There has been much pessimistic talk in Scottish literary circles of a poetic recession following upon the boom years of the forties and fifties. Believing that this was a publishing rather than a poetic depression we launched the poetry magazine *Akros*. Now as a further expression of this belief we are publishing a series of collections by individual poets – the "Akros Poets".' The title of the series led, however, to confusion with the magazine and although we were confirmed by the warm reception given to *Soundings* and *Two and Two Make One* in our belief that there was a need, and a demand, for such pamphlets, I abandoned the series title when I published our next pamphlet in May 1967. It was a group collection of *Poems* by Alan Hayton, Stephen Mulrine, Colin Kirkwood and Robert Tait edited by Edwin Morgan who knew them as students at Glasgow University. This was their first collection. The most enduring and the most famous poem in this pamphlet must be Stephen Mulrine's much-anthologised 'The Coming of the Wee Malkies' which I would quote despite its being so well-known:

Whit'll ye dae when the wee Malkies come,
if they dreep doon affy the wash-hoose dyke,
and pit the hems oan the sterrheid light,
an play wee heidies oan the clean close-wa,
an blooter yir windae in wi the baw,
missis, whit'll ye dae?

Whit'll ye dae when the wee Malkies come,
if they chap yir door, an choke yir drains,
an caw the feet far yir sapsy weans,
an tummle thur wulkies through yir sheets,
an tim thur ashes oot in the street,
missis, whit'll ye dae?

Whit'll ye dae when the wee Malkies come,
if they chuck thur screwtaps doon the pan,
an stick the heid oan the sanit'ry man;
when ye hear thum shauchlin doon yir loaby,
chantin, 'Wee Malkies! The gemme's a bogey!'
– Haw, missis, whit'll ye dae?

Our next pamphlet was another first collection, *Thunder in the Air* by Stewart Conn. Although the texts of these pamphlets were printed by Lloyds, I continued to hand-print the covers; my wife and I hand-gathered the texts and she hand-sewed the covers on. Indeed, I was still intending to continue printing *Akros* magazine myself and got new type for No. 5 – Times New Roman – although the old Baskerville was used for some of the poems. For No. 5 we also got some good quality paper – Basingwerk – and introduced a new tall narrow shape. It was published in June 1967 and sold out almost overnight and is one of the now rare issues of *Akros*. This proved, however, to be the end of our hand-letterpress printing apart from covers, stationery, and the pamphlet printing of my *Idols* as we were given a Scottish Arts Council grant for *Akros* from No. 6 which was printed by Lloyds, and showed a big stride forward in that it was increased to fifty-six pages and printed lengthy prose pieces as well as poetry.

With *Akros* 6 we are at December 1967 but earlier in that year I had been really venturing out although never going beyond the money available to pay printers' bills, but perhaps risking more than I could afford to lose. The Glasgow poets, as I have said, were published in May and in June I published not only Stewart Conn and my *Idols* but also Iain Crichton Smith's much-admired but controversial essay on MacDiarmid, *The Golden Lyric*, which attracted a lot of reviews and sold very well.

In August I published a book on which I had risked all my money resources in a fine piece of printing to honour Hugh MacDiarmid on his seventy-fifth birthday – *Poems Addressed to Hugh MacDiarmid* which I edited. It printed poems addressed to MacDiarmid by a wide range of poets which were written over many years. It is a limited edition of 350 numbered copies quarter-bound in leather with hand-made Japanese paper to cover the boards. The text paper is Glaston-bury Antique Laid from Abbey Mills. From the beginning I had only one man in mind as printer and that was Thomas Rae of Greenock, well-known for his Signet Press. I was fortunate in that he was willing to take on the book. I designed it, there were portraits of MacDiarmid by Leonard Penrice, and Compton Mackenzie wrote a preface. All the copies were signed by me as editor and by Leonard Penrice, and the first fifty copies were also signed by all the contributing poets and the printer, which makes a very interesting page of signatures.

I had an interesting time visiting some of the poets to get their signatures. I am not likely to forget the demonstration of Norman MacCaig's incisive mind in a long conversation I had with him. Nor will I forget Sydney Goodsir Smith's reluctance to sign the sheets rather early in the morning. And how can I forget the kindness of Helen

Cruickshank who put me up for the night in her Corstorphine home where so many famous Scottish literary people have stayed. Nor will I forget my first introduction to Alexander Scott's sharp wit, nor to T. S. Law's fine conversation, with his two, then schoolboy, sons listening so intently. I also remember well Leonard Penrice and myself sitting upstairs in my spare bedroom/print room signing all the copies. I remember too the day the Penrices and I spent at MacDiarmid's home whilst Leonard did the drawings for the book.

In all copies of *Poems Addressed to Hugh MacDiarmid* is a list of subscribers which I really slaved getting, although I need not have worked so hard as the book was over-subscribed and is now fetching high prices – £45 for the ordinary copies which I sold to subscribers for £3 3/-. Still I did write – by hand – hundreds of letters asking people to subscribe and I was exhausted by the end of my campaign. Fortunately I had recovered somewhat before the party I gave in Glasgow at which I presented Hugh MacDiarmid with the first copy. This party was a huge, and very crowded, success although MacDiarmid used his speech to attack the newly announced magazine *Scottish International*, including Edwin Morgan who was associated with it and also had a poem in *Poems Addressed to Hugh MacDiarmid*. But after Norman MacCaig had excellently read some of the poems MacDiarmid made a second and more mellow speech.

I was not finished, however, for 1967 and in October I published George Bruce's *Landscapes and Figures*, another book that soon sold out. It was George Bruce's first collection of poems since his *Selected Poems* published twenty years earlier in 1947 and I suggested the idea of a book to him at the party Chambers gave to launch my *Hugh MacDiarmid and the Scottish Renaissance*. Since 1967 George Bruce has shown how much poetry he wrote in these blank publishing years with the publication, by Edinburgh University Press, of his excellent *Collected Poems* (1970).

December 1967 saw the delivery to us of the flat sheets of the new fat *Akros* 6 and although it was a pleasure to receive them fully printed we, my wife and I, had to gather them and she had to sew them into the covers which is a job to give anyone sore fingers, not to mention the state of deep boredom which it induces. This gathering and sewing we continued to do right up to No. 14 and we not only did the gathering again for Nos. 16 and 17 but my wife also typed them onto stencils and printed them on a Gestetner duplicating (not litho) machine which we had just bought. By then it was a big job and I'll never forget these huge piles of paper as we gathered them. They went down so very slowly. Numbers 16 and 17 were 'perfect' bound by Sanderson's the binders of Preston, another family company, run by Frank Sanderson, with whom I had a very happy business relationship. So far as I know no reader of *Akros* has ever complained of the quality of the binding. But at a personal level I will never forget the pleasure and the anticipation of another issue delivered as Sanderson's van arrived, usually after I had returned from work about six o'clock, at 14 Parklands Avenue, Penwortham, Preston.

It was only from No. 18 that the printing and gathering and binding were all done commercially, giving us the pleasure of the delivery of complete copies, although by No. 18 despatching subscription and bookshop copies had become, and remained to the end, a big job in itself. I took the early issues of the magazine to the Post Office in my daughter's large pram and later in a wheelbarrow. I was still doing this in the late seventies when we first moved to Radcliffe-on-Trent. I got some strange looks from passers-by and people who know that I wheelbarrowed *Akros* find this fact amusing although I thought nothing of it as I went back and forward between our house and the Post Office. When we moved to our second house in Radcliffe we were too far from a Post Office for wheelbarrowing and subscription and bookshop copies were taken in a very overloaded taxi.

In October 1982 *Akros* reached its fiftieth issue and to accompany it I edited and published an anthology entitled *Akros Verse 1965-1982*. This is a collection of fifty poems – each by a different poet – from the first forty-nine issues of *Akros*, in celebration of fifty issues. It shows, I believe, how much good poetry has appeared in the magazine and how wide has been the range of poetry. This anthology is the 110th item published by me, with all the numbers of *Akros* counted as only one item, and it is not without a little pride that I state these statistics, considering our small beginnings all these years ago in Hemel Hempstead in 1962 although, as I have said, the full name of Akros Publications was not used until after we moved to Penwortham, Preston, in 1965.

In an interview in *Akros* 50 (October 1982) I was asked which poem springs first into my mind when I think of the first forty-nine numbers of *Akros*. The interview continued:

D.G.: Well again that's another competitive game that I don't much like.

M.I.: But with your memories of *Akros* one or two poems must immediately come to mind.

D.G.: Yes they do. I think immediately of two poems by Alex Scott – his 'To Mourn Jayne Mansfield' and 'Dear Deid Dancer'. I think of groups of poems by Alastair Mackie that later appeared in *Clytach*. I think of Robert Garioch's now famous poem 'At Robert Fergusson's Grave' which was printed in the very first *Akros*. I think, to be honest and naturally enough, of some of my own poems – 'My Faither' and 'Innocence' and so on. I think of Edwin Morgan's 'Glasgow Green' and I have a real attachment to Iain Crichton Smith's 'For Ann in America in the Autumn' although I don't think Iain has reprinted it. I think of Maurice Lindsay's 'Toward Light' and his 'Stones in Sky and Water'. I think of George Bruce's 'Single Ticket'. I think of Liz Lochhead's 'Her Place' and of Tom Leonard's 'Feed Ma Lamz'. And so I could go on pulling poems out of my memory. But you've seen the anthology of fifty poems by fifty poets that I have edited to go with *Akros* 50 and these are fifty of the many poems I remember. Of course I also remember poems printed in books and pamphlets outside *Akros* magazine but published by Akros Publications.

M.I.: You've published more than a hundred books and pamphlets. Which of them do you remember best? Or which are your favourites?

D.G.: Again a small publisher remembers all his books but I suppose I remember three with most excitement and pleasure; Alexander Scott's *Cantrips*, Alastair Mackie's *Clytach* and my own *In Appearances*.

M.I.: You seem definite enough about that.

D.G.: Yes, but now I think of all the others I'm pleased with. But many are less important because they are less unique – less important in a publishing sense. For instance I think George Bruce's *Landscapes and Figures* a fine book that needed publishing after all the years when we had had no new books of poetry from George, but it was superseded by the EUP *The Collected Poems of George Bruce*. Really the best poems in *Landscapes* would have appeared only a little later in the Edinburgh volume. Maurice Lindsay's *This Business of Living* was a book I put a lot of work into and it is important to me as its publisher, but Maurice has had so many books published since then that it now seems but one of many in his list of books. So also I am proud of Alexander Scott's *Selected Poems 1943-1974* and I believe it did – and continues to do – a necessary publishing job, but because it is a 'Selected Poems' it is less pioneering as a publishing venture than his *Cantrips*. My own publications which came after *In Appearances*, such as *Mr & Mrs J. L. Stoddart* or *Buits and Wellies* or *Gaitherings* or *Realities Poems* or *On Midsummer Evenin Merriest of Nichts?* are very important to me, but I was an old hand at publishing when they appeared whereas *In Appearances* was quite early.

M.I.: From what you wrote in *Forward from Hugh MacDiarmid* you are obviously not going to forget Flora Garry's *Bennygoak*.

D.G.: Indeed not; that was certainly a case of a book taking off and, in poetry terms, becoming a bestseller. Alexander Scott's anthology *Modern Scots Verse 1922-1977* is another important piece of editing and publishing I think. I also think that publishing two novels by John

Herdman was important. If *A Truth Lover* or *Pagan's Pilgrimage* had come earlier in our publishing 'history' I'm sure I'd have them in my best-remembered list.

M.I.: The Parklands Poets series was very important surely for putting into print our new or unpublished poets.

D.G.: Yes, although they are not all unknowns – Alex Scott and Edwin Morgan appear in the series.

The book by Alexander Scott in the Parklands Poets series is *Greek Fire* and as well as his *Cantrips* and *Selected Poems 1943-1974* we also published his *Double Agent* where his now famous group of two-liners were first collected under the title 'Scotched'. I would end this chapter by quoting two of them which are on subjects which Alex Scott and I both know a lot about, although he has more direct experience of the former than I have:

SCOTCH EDUCATION

I tell't ye
I tell't ye

SCOTCH POETS

Wha's the
T'ither?

CHAPTER 15

Whaur Scottish Poets Are Met

D ESPITE Alex Scott's poem at the end of the last chapter, both he and I have known many Scottish poets. But although I have been so closely involved with poets I have never really socialised with them regularly although I suppose I have met and spoken to most of the better known ones at some time or another. However, I have never been part of the Edinburgh literary pub scene although I have been in all the famous pubs. There is a section in my *In Appearances* which gives an outsider's view of some aspects of this drinking *literati*. Some people have assumed from the section I quote below that I know it well but, as I say, I know it only as an outsider and occasional visitor, and to be honest I do not see excessive drinking as a sign of a good literary life in a city. But each to his own, so long as it does not destroy other people. But my poem is not, I hope, as serious as I have just been in writing the above sentences.

A LAD O PAIRTS II

Me . . . me . . .
Aa o a trummle and deaf and dumb
to aa the baur-flees swarmin owre
thae weill-kent freends swammin
and doublin round afore my een.

Time's aa here.
Or's shut up shop.

Aa thae shut in lands and lums
aff the High Street or Royal Mile
whaur hing the stink o past and slums;
here whaur Hume and Boswell still
for me a *literati* livin in proper style.

A makar staunin straucht and upricht
on savin shelves wha's perjink words
are slaw crabbit waffie beasties
beilin in aa the pairts o mysel.

A haingin the faiple sat dribblin
owre a braw muffler and waistcoat
wi fancy talk and learnit freends
noddin owre the *eau de vie*.

And the Coogate aneath aa notice
or, atmaist, guid for a lauch
the wey they cairry on wi meth, and the polis
efter tarts aa for taen the jaicket aff
your back – and mair! And no for a lauch!

And that smoother toun that cares
(though New they caa it yet!)
for its Offices and auld Adam squares.
And Rose Street; a gallus gett
whaur e'en livin Scottish poets are met.

A lang bouky hash-a-pie. Aye
the loud and cheerie blethersket
kennin aabody and aye sinkin lang
dram for dram wi skeerie haunds.

Pubs aawhaur! Abbotsford there
and Milne's wi its photos o MacDiarmid,
MacCaig, S. G. Smith – and mair;
and still there's Paddy's, and them hid
frae tourists and aa the unco guid.

A hauchlin theeveless gommerill
aye at hame in the Abbotsford
or the Goth; slaverin in a gless
and greedy for her hingin owre.

A bent dominie neat wi a perchment
aa signed by the Education folk
giein pouer to teach them bent
on passin on to be a lad o pairts.

Eenity, feenity, fickity, fay
Ell, dell, domin ay,
Urky, burky, stoory rock
An tan toosy Jock.

A dowie, doitit dottle playin
the lad o aa the pairts.

Aa the pairts!
Aa the pairts
frae me mysel.

There *is* I and you.

And there's them
I wouldna be haein
at hame
– wi me.

CHAPTER 16

For the New

FROM No. 6, December 1967, until the final issue, No. 52, in October 1983, *Akros* was a fully professional magazine in that, thanks to Scottish Arts Council grants and a very loyal list of subscribers, there was the money to allow me a lot of scope in editing it, and also in advertising it and generally getting it known. There are, of course, some numbers which have become quite famous. No. 7 is a Norman MacCaig issue, No. 10 a Sydney Goodsir Smith issue, No. 47 an Edwin Muir issue, and there have been two special Hugh MacDiarmid double issues. The first of these, published in April 1970, attracted a lot of attention and sold out very quickly. It was perhaps especially of interest, from what people have said to me, for the printing of the long illustrated conversation I had with MacDiarmid, at his cottage, Broomsbank, on 25th October 1968. This conversation was illustrated not only by photographs taken during and after our conversation by three photographers from Preston Polytechnic – Arthur Thompson, Jim Bamber and Geoff Green – but also by early previously unpublished photographs of MacDiarmid as a young man and indeed also as a baby with his mother and father. The publication of these early photographs was quite a scoop. The photographers and I had a memorable time at MacDiarmid's home that day in October 1968 and the conversation has become quite famous and is still much in demand despite a separate pamphlet printing of it which also sold out very quickly. In his essay 'In Memory of MacDiarmid' in *Aquarius* 11, 1979, G. S. Fraser kindly wrote: 'A more vivid impression of the man, by one who knew him much better, is to be found in a splendid recorded conversation with one of his staunchest supporters in his later years, Duncan Glen of *Akros*'. In a letter to me dated 27th March 1970 MacDiarmid wrote: 'the photos came up splendidly – particularly the older ones which I hardly expected to reproduce so well or perhaps at all'.

But in addition to these numbers which featured individual poets, there were other special issues: a translation issue which attracted a lot of praise; a visual issue which was attacked and praised in equal measure but is still much sought after; a Sicilian-Scottish issue; a criticism of American poets number; an Anti-Lit number which inflamed Scottish traditionalists; a long poem issue; a criticism of poetry issue which was also attacked by traditionalists; a Gaelic issue; several Scots language issues. In addition to these special issues the more general ones carried many long essays on individual poets' work which built up into what I believe to be a very fine and extensive analysis of twentieth-century Scottish poetry in Scots and English. I think I celebrated well with No. 50 not least for a new departure for *Akros*; a photographic sequence by Euan Duff who is on the staff of my department at Trent Polytechnic. I was also indebted to other colleagues at both Preston and Trent for designs and drawings for covers – George Hollingworth did several and David Hearn and John Oldfield did one each. Others were done by Preston students although overall I did most of the covers myself as I also did the overall design.

I also think No. 51 a pleasing ending to the life of *Akros* with fine poetry and interesting criticism including twenty short essays by twenty critics on twenty famous twentieth-century Scottish poems. It was no easy task getting all these essays in on time but well worth the effort to judge by correspondents' reaction to them. Of the poetry in *Akros* 51 it gave me much pleasure to have a group of poems by Alastair Mackie which showed him once again breaking ground new to him. Alastair appeared in the first number and so it was a real pleasure to have poetry by him in the final issue. I was also very pleased to print extracts from a long sequence 'Dundee Doldrums' by W. N. Herbert a young poet making his first appearance on the Scottish poetry scene. In my editorial I wrote that Bill Herbert's sequence 'could prove to be as important a work as any that has appeared in *Akros* and it is only one section of a very long poem in progress'. It is splendid that work such as this should appear just as *Akros* finishes. The Scots tradition is still alive and Bill Herbert is certainly attempting to 'make it new'. The other poet by whom I printed an extended group of poems in the last *Akros* was Margaret Gillies and I believe her to be a fine poet who has not received the recognition she deserves on the Scottish poetry scene. I am sad to leave the printing of these and many other fine poets to others but a void is always filled if the demand is there for it to be filled. I am confident that Scottish poets will make that demand and that a new editor will appear to respond to it.

I would like to think that there was quite a lot of humour in *Akros*. I also like to think that some of our advertising was at least slightly witty, although, as one of our brochures said, we could also blow our own trumpet as in this statement on a page from that same brochure: '*Akros* has, of course, attracted some abuse as well as much praise. Alan Bold generously wrote: "*Akros* 4 creaks with the bored attitudinising of its contributors though *Akros* 5 is a great improvement typographically and artistically. It had to be." But before very long we were reading

Tom Scott: "*Akros* has easily established itself as by far the best Scottish poetry magazine for decades; it has no rival in sight". And many others have followed with kind remarks. "*Akros* has established itself as one of the great magazines of our time; a magazine filled with the real meat of poetry, of good literature." "*Akros* is certainly a good magazine." "One of the great literary magazines of these islands in the past ten years." "It has certainly been a remarkable achievement on the part of the indefatigable Duncan Glen." "The most attractive, visually, of all the publications sponsored by the Scottish Arts Council." "Scotland's most lively literary journal." And finally for the benefit of George Hollingworth, our illustrator, I quote Peter Finch describing *Akros* as "The Scottish giant thundering on...".' In the brochure our illustrator drew a rather uncouth giant in boilersuit passing two natty gents, one of whom is saying, 'There he goes thundering'.

With the end of the 'giant' *Akros* I started in December 1983 a very different kind of magazine which is small, free and limited to one hundred copies. I have given it the title *Aynd* which is the old Scots word for breath.

The fact that the first issue of *Akros* to be devoted to a single poet was No. 7 on Norman MacCaig shows how highly I rate his work. Other long essays on his poetry appeared later in the magazine. But I do not admire MacCaig only as a poet. I admire the movement of his intellect in conversation as in his poetry or literary criticism – indeed in all that he does. I admire the way he does not pander to accepted ideas of how a poet of national standing should react to situations such as interviews. I admire his stand against sentimentality or soft-centred thinking or action. Time and again his poetry has surprised me. And yet in the Introduction to my *The Akros Anthology of Scottish Poetry 1965-70* I took it upon myself to attack his poetry and to suggest presumptuously new directions which his poetry could take. He quite understandably took great offence at this and although he continued to subscribe to *Akros* he did not thereafter send me poems for it. In the Introduction to the anthology I also pointed to new paths that I thought Edwin Morgan could take as a poet and yet I also greatly admire his poetry and have shown this not only by regularly publishing poems by him in *Akros* but also by publishing two pamphlets of poems by him under the Akros Publications imprint and by printing a long interview with him in *Akros* as well as two long essays on his poetry.

I would like now to look at what I was attempting to do in that controversial Introduction and to look at the situation of Scottish poetry at that time.

From 1965, when I founded *Akros*, until 1969, when I wrote my

Introduction to the anthology, Scottish poetry was still suffering from the influence of the anti-Scots propaganda which arose in the late fifties and early sixties as a reaction to the previous years when Hugh MacDiarmid and his Scots-writing disciples were dominant influences upon the Scottish poetry scene. The years 1965-69 and, indeed, the years 1959-69 (which were covered by Norman MacCaig and Alexander Scott's anthology *Contemporary Scottish Verse*) saw two influences dominant. Firstly there was Norman MacCaig and his many younger followers working in what I had rather rudely called the polite English tradition. Secondly there had been (slightly later) the emergence of the non-polite poets who showed the influence of the American poets who have carried on after William Carlos Williams and the Black Mountain poets. In 1969 I believed that despite a Scottish subject content to some of their work almost all of these poets had their eyes directed to outside Scotland. I saw them involved in the Scottish literary scene and perhaps initially establishing themselves through the Scottish little magazines or through Scottish readings or through Scottish small press publishing. Finally, however, I suggested, they looked to non-Scottish editorial and critical sources for recognition. I believed that they wished to please English editors and publishers and this I suggested was destructive to poetry in Scotland. I saw us being in danger of moving back to a situation where the literary capital of Scotland was London. I believed that the achievement – richly deserved – of Norman MacCaig in showing that a Scottish writer can achieve a London publishing success without leaving Edinburgh had been part of this decline back towards the pre-MacDiarmid position. Since the end of World War Two we had also had a return to the '*belles lettres* atmosphere' which MacDiarmid had effectively destroyed in the twenties and thirties. Also I believed, and indeed still do, that by looking to London we are in great danger of becoming imitators and providers of second-rate goods aimed at a market previously created in London – we become craftsmen, not creators.

I saw Scottish poets complaining about the lack of native publishers but, once established, few of them were casting in their lot with the small Scottish publishers who could grow larger, and yet, I believed, as long as there is a lack of native publishers the Scottish poet can be tempted by the need to give London what it wants, and so the Scottish poet can remain in danger of being an imitation English or English-American poet. The Scottish poet has to have the true independence to accept foreign influences whilst remaining true to himself and perhaps one of the first essentials of this is the establishment of native critical standards as those to which Scottish poets look for acceptance. So long as a London acceptance is considered superior (by Scots) to an

Edinburgh, Glasgow or Inverness or Aberdeen one then Scottish culture is far from healthy. From my stance in 1969 or 1970 this seemed a real and growing danger.

And then, as a good controversialist, I turned to two of the most important of the Scottish poets who write in English – MacCaig and Morgan. I wrote in the Introduction.

'During the five years under consideration the English-writing poets have progressed rather as might be expected, although Norman MacCaig raised my hopes highly when he moved into free forms. Somehow MacCaig, for all the professional admiration a poet can give to his skill as a maker of verses, has almost always had too much conscious control of his poetry; the whole man does not seem to push through into the verse. Edwin Morgan has been seemingly much more adventurous in exploring verse forms and to me his *The Second Life* was the most interesting new English collection of the last five years, but yet I believe also that with his work, as with MacCaig's there is a self-restraining self-consciousness or puritanism underlying even the most experimental of his poetry. The technical skills and controls of MacCaig and Morgan hitched to the wild horses of passionate living language – that would indeed give us a new Scottish poetry. Professor Butter, writing sympathetically of that earlier practitioner in English, Edwin Muir, suggested that for all Muir's success in English (and Professor Butter linked Norman MacCaig with Muir as another successful Scottish poet writing in English) 'It is possible that he might have been able to put more colour into his work if he had been able to use the same language as he had heard spoken around him in youth'. (*Edwin Muir*, Writers and Critics Series, 1962). I feel the same with regard to both MacCaig and Morgan although there arises the question of why they have avoided making poetry out of the language they know rather than the language they have learned as, unlike Muir, they remain resident in the areas of their birth. All this is a question not of versifying skills or cleverness with ideas (craft and cleverness have never been enough in poetry writing) but of the underlying power of language. Both poets obviously have this power but, for me, it is tamed except in short bursts as in Edwin Morgan's 'Glasgow Green' poem, although I enjoy it intellectually as I intellectually enjoy the skills of both poets. But intellectual appreciation is not enough for us to say that this is truly important poetry.'

Now, more than ten years on, the cultural climate is more relaxed, as am I, although there are still plenty of people willing to suggest that poetry in Scots is on the way out. Also, of course, I am older and wiser and I can see that perhaps Norman MacCaig and Edwin Morgan had created literary languages which are based on the speech they learned

as children in their parents' homes. Perhaps the Scots vocabulary
element in their natural speech has always been slight. Anyway what
counts is the poetry and not theories about language, and the importance of their poetry is undeniable although I believe both of them have
extended their range since I wrote in 1969. This is not to reject their
earlier work. Indeed it may be that *Riding Lights*, published in 1955,
remains my favourite single book by Norman MacCaig although his
Selected Poems is indispensable and we urgently need a 'Collected
Poems'.* We also need a full-length critical book. And I do not with-
draw my praise of Edwin Morgan's *The Second Life* given in my
Introduction.

But I attacked not only MacCaig and Morgan and indeed looking
back it was the influence of MacCaig which I as an editor saw in scores
of poems by mini-MacCaigs dropping through the *Akros* letterbox that
I was really attacking – not, of course, that MacCaig can be blamed
for his imitators. The Introduction continues:

'I have concentrated on Messrs MacCaig and Morgan as they are
the most important English-writing poets, but the same criticisms
can, I believe, be levelled at those other poets who have followed
knowingly or unknowingly the example of MacCaig or Morgan.
Personally I feel more optimistic about the work of those – the
Scottish Redskins – who have looked, like Edwin Morgan, to
America rather than those Palefaces who have looked, like
MacCaig, to the polite English tradition or to academicism, al-
though, of course, it can be argued that MacCaig is a polite
Scottish-English Wallace Stevens. The most notable younger
Scottish Redskin who has emerged is Alan Jackson and of the
Palefaces obviously Iain Crichton Smith stands out with the
human commitment in his work distinguishing him from Norman
MacCaig and more obviously from those who have followed
MacCaig whilst lacking both the sharp edge of his mind and his
poetic skills. Stewart Conn also demands mention and younger
English-writing poets perhaps influenced by MacCaig who have
appeared even more recently include Laughton Johnston and
James Rankin. Outside the MacCaig sphere stands George
Mackay Brown who is the one obvious omission from the pages of
Akros and Akros Publications and so, sadly, from this anthology.
Equally distinctive amongst the younger poets is D. M. Black and
a more recently-emerged poet of individual promise is Roderick
Watson.'

But I also thought the Scots movement needed prodding and wrote:

'If recently too many young poets writing in English have been
too-easily content to follow the example of MacCaig or of the

* Published since this was written.

post-Carlos Williams Americans, so also too many of these writings in Scots have been content to continue in the established Scottish Renaissance traditions. It has become too easy to follow MacDiarmid or the second wave of Renaissance poets – Sydney Goodsir Smith, Robert Garioch, Alexander Scott, Tom Scott. The poets writing in English who have looked to London or America or Liverpool have at least believed themselves to be forward-looking whereas *until recently* too many writers in Scots have been easily content to accept the present conditions – which really meant looking back. Writing of Scots poetry in a review of *Scottish Poetry* 4, Douglas Gifford suggested: "The successes and the limitations of Scots poetry seem to be pretty much the same since Ramsay. The necessary stride into all the affairs of twentieth-century Scots, let alone the world, hasn't taken place . . . although in *Cantrips* Alexander Scott got as close as anyone in his poems on Isadora Duncan and on the death of Jayne Mansfield to using Scots in this desired way . . ." Mr Gifford underestimates the achievment of MacDiarmid by referring back to Ramsay, but there is no doubt that this step is an essential to Scots poetry. It is a step which I believe is now being taken. It is not clear from Mr Gifford's necessarily compressed review whether he recognises that this step has little or nothing to do with subject content; it has to do with a use of language and with the expression of a new sensibility and with a new awareness created and turned fully new by the imagination. It is the step out of romanticism and dualism into a modern nominalist position. It is, as yet, truly expressible only in poetry but a primary quality of this new sensibility is an ever-moving acceptance of the only reality as existing within our own newly-created fields of knowledge – in a new space and time. I have written more fully of this in oblique-angled essays in *Akros* but here I can quote only Carlos Williams who spoke for all of us aware of our new accepting oneness when he stated: "I knew all – it became me". As did Wallace Stevens: "the giant of nothingness, each one/And the giant everchanging, living in change". That acceptance and new awareness is what Scots poetry has to step into and what I believe it is now attempting to step into. The signs of this change or stride forward can be seen in the recent poetry of Alastair Mackie. Compare the Scots poems in the early issues of *Akros* with those in No. 12 and those which are about to be printed in No. 15 as I write. I reprint all eight of his poems from *Akros* 12 in this anthology and a comparison can be made with the excellent, but earlier, 'Still Life – Cézanne' which I also print. The importance of Alastair Mackie, an Aberdonian living in Anstruther, will be seen even more clearly in an important collection of his Scots poems which Akros Publications plan to publish in 1971, entitled *Clytach*.'

That Introduction was primarily concerned with promoting

developments in Scottish poetry and particularly with encouraging the then early signs of a third wave of writers in Scots. But I was also attempting to advance my theories of this 'new nominalist' poetry. I rather foisted this theory onto the poetry of Alastair Mackie as well as onto my own and Alastair did not really accept my theorising, which is not to say that I was not correct in seeing the new sensibility of the imagination in his poetry. In my Introduction I put the emphasis on 'making new' rather than on 'traditionalism' although they are dependent one upon the other. Certainly when my long four-part sequence 'John Atman' was first published in my *Kythings*, 1969, I was pleased to see Roderick Watson write in a review in *Catalyst* (Spring 1970) that 'for the most part this laconic and allusive sequence presents us with a new and creatively positive handling of the Scots tradition'. 'John Atman' is part of *In Appearances* which was published by Akros Publications in 1971. Alastair Mackie's *Clytach*, referred to above, duly appeared in 1972 and we had previously published Alexander Scott's *Cantrips* which Douglas Gifford referred to in my quotation above. It is my immodest belief that these three books published by Akros Publications – *Cantrips, In Appearances* and *Clytach* – ushered in a new movement in poetry in Scots. Alexander Scott's work is, of course, also part of the second wave of Scots-writing poets, but he is also perhaps the link with the third which was heralded, I believe, by *In Appearances* and *Clytach* and was continued by such writers as Donald Campbell, Walter Perrie and William Findlay and is being further continued by newer writers including Christopher Rush, Raymond Vettese, Raymond Falconer and W. N. Herbert. The first wave of Renaissance Scots-writing poets can be seen to be essentially MacDiarmid and William Soutar and the second wave to be Sydney Goodsir Smith, Robert Garioch, Alexander Scott, Tom Scott and T. S. Law, to be very selective; a fine group of poets collectively continuing the Scots tradition in poetry, but when I wrote my Introduction to *The Akros Anthology of Scottish Poetry 1965-70* I felt, as I have said, that I had to speak out for new developments. Also, as a poet, I felt rather alone which no doubt explains, in some degree, the somewhat harsh (and perhaps unfair) tone of the piece. But I do not apologise for it even if I regret the rift with Norman MacCaig whom I admire so much as man and poet which may, with Scottish cussedness, be the reason I criticised his work so severely. I think it was necessary in its time and with different personalities it has been necessary again. No doubt it will be necessary in the future as we (or our successors) struggle for the new.

CHAPTER 17

John Atman

IN THE last chapter I referred to my sequence of poems *In Appearances* and to the final section of that book 'John Atman'. That final section is a part of my writing which gives me personally much pleasure and I was very pleased when Nat Scammacca, who translated a lot of *In Appearances* into Italian, translated the whole of 'John Atman' and had his version printed in the Sicilian paper *Trapani Nuova* (September 1974). He also printed his version of the full length of 'John Atman', without telling me, in the anthology *La Nuova Poesia Scozzese* (Celebes Editore, 1976) which we edited together. In the middle seventies I sometimes thought the sequence was better appreciated in Sicily than in Scotland. In a letter to *Akros* (No. 28, August 1975) the 'Poets of Sicily' very kindly wrote of me as 'the fine poet of "John Atman" (one of the truly important literary achievements in this second half of the twentieth-century). We Sicilian poets know this poem now, from beginning to end – and, for us it is Scotland.' I print 'John Atman' here partly because of its autobiographical form but, although I draw on some of my personal experiences in it, it is, unlike this prose work, an 'imaginary' autobiography.

JOHN ATMAN

I

This is daurk Lanarkshire
sae I hae learnt.
But we ken aye there
a land o sun and blue skies.
A time o lang days and play
wi my brithers.
We desire only
the cool blue watter.

Here the river glintles.
A past gaein slow;
the watter black agin the gress
cool ablow the risin
waves o heat. And our faither
lazy
in the warm shade.

And the wun there
wi warmth afore its waves;
and aye she moves
ahint aa our play
a brichtness shut in the gairden
– and heavy wi fruit.

Watter rinnin slaw in thochts
toom ablow the sky. Days
at ease wi our brithers
and aa o yird and kin
in their ways.

And the corn there. Fenced
by our faither. Yellowin ears
on lang stalks that move us
toward the hairst for days
our faither fears.
We desire only
the cool blue watter.

Happy in her they gaither fruit
hidden frae us. Bricht-haired dochter.
His child. And aa time
in our mither. Their child
in her airms. We staun alane
and canna see
without dank borders.

Growths spreidin, creepin, rinnin
green frae the sile. The smile
frae deep drainin rutes and yird;
and cauld hauns seen
crossed
that early ee'nin.

Our gairden is shut
wi her gane; white. Her dochter
bides bricht as the fruit
in that ripe gairden
o the days afore the corn was
laid and the straw cut.

Our faither cut grey wi pain
and cauld. His lang-baned body
live wi knowledge
o days spent,
and sleep shut in the gairden
though the paths are
open

and the auld trees
in blossom that hauds nae stain.

The blossom calls. The gairden
our mither returns to
wi the strength o his winter.
Days for which she nourishes
strange sons. Their weys forced
outside trig lairs.
And soon
growe strong and broun
and faither wi them
nourished to their hairst.

II

In my thochts daurk corners
and unkent steps.
Journeys across swung stairweys.
Across daurk rivers on brigs
felt wi streekit fingers;
open weys wi missin steps
and sweyin haunrails shadows
saft and grey agin the nicht.

A time o closed roads and unkent
fields. Great daurk acres
shut out by quick faain hills
and sma halls o endless dance.

A spring held ticht; and wound
to the grip o innocence. A spring
vibratin as he walks
a challenge
to his brithers. A time o unwindin
to ithers' time.

A large stride across a street.
The hidden selves safe aneath
quick thrustin strides. Unheard
voices drouned in the blood
racin. A time o lookin
frae ahint an unshaved face.

White strangers rise uncalled
frae the licht
across the broun-rigged field
and welcomin striae.
Bricht-haired shadows rinnin

through our nicht; shairp wi
unkent knives cutting across
the raw stane. And the beat o haimmers
edgin to brittle pairts
that spairk quick, and chip
against unseen heids. A time
o shairp corners and short cuts
taen blin.

The stane rises daurk against
the sky. And a table is set
across a field.

And the fast days by the sea.
A time o cheek and sichts.
A pride in being seen.
A time o talk and challenge.
Great proud trophies
walkt doun a street
and cairrit back in talk.

Great journeys taen across
ither fields open to ither lichts;
great doins imagined
and fulfilled in acts o talk.
We walk out loudly in
saft shoes
scornin the sea
and the lang-legged dochters;
a time for lauchter and nonsense
and great facts in rough houses
staunin against the sea.

A great voice salt against
the weathered waa. And turnin
a grey face to smile faur out
to sma boats risin
at buoys. A time o bricht
daurkness and haurd gless tables
set wi hauf-filled bottles.

And the dance. Heids on a hidden
floor. A turnin licht movin
through the spectrum. The warm
wi the cool. A sad yellow
and a turnin green. Heild ticht
on sprung boards. Turn and turn
again. The great springs taut
in ithers' haunds.

Great gaitherings o dochters
turnin. The owre-lookin.
And the dance. Close and fast
turnin steps. Time and time again
round movin limbs. Quick steps
and slaw movements. Gyrations
full and round wi the beat
time and time again.

Tall slow steps; quick turnin
heids and quait talk. And the hame-
takin
by the sea.

The sea against the stanes.
A breakwatter ablow the street.
And large steps unner watter
black and live wi the broken
lichts
stretchin across the bay
calm ayont the risin stane,
sandbanks and crustit rocks.

III

Bricht polished windows
and flowering trees. Quiet days
by tall grey houses safe
high up the hill. And long days
warm on slopin rocks
watchin small waves turning
far out on furrowed
sand.

And blue skies above the pool
lazy wi sleepin dochters
and their friends
undisturbed.

Days of blue seas safe
on this sea front. Waves swept
doun grilled drains. And grey couples
watchin frae shelters.
Round walks by fields still green
and safe
frae combine or mill wheels.

And licht ev'nins owrelookin
cherry trees and firm lawns . . .

She walks pink and cool
doun stairs and through doors,
dress swingin owre uneven
streets; across green paths,
and small blue ponds wi dookin birds
bricht wi greens and blues;
bricht mallards and dull ducks
paddlin ablow a pentit bridge
railed wi smooth worn planks.

And gates are open; the park roads
lined
wi saft gas lichts
owre safe hills
and testit bridges
owrehung
wi willows we hide in alane
above the unseen watter. And sma
quick steps doun earth paths
to round rows
and the baun-staun
sad wi litter and past concerts.

And run. And run.
And run and climb that hill
high owre grey tours and hingin
reek. Saintly churches but
lines
against the sky and learnit
spires a pettern raisin us
thegither against the nicht.

A time of hame-comin and visitin
hame. New faces in auld.
And strength ahint closed doors
and rung bells.

The warmth is in us. We lie
thegither;
the fields are sma
and licht frae our gairden. The days
are lazy and fou wi the trees
growin ablow us. And she walks doun,
and full-skirtit, wi warmth
and fear by his side. Waitin
and growein
life.

A stranger. A time of confinement
and doors closin. Of waitin

and walkin. A time of sleep.
Of climbin close stairs
– and cauld. He rises
across the sky. Heavy clouds
blowin through the park. And gates
are closin. We wait on time.

The tide in her strong and high
wi waves that rise
and fall ayont the swingin
wecht. A flood rode dry
outside the ark braithless and
strong in her blood. That knot
made to untie. And turn
in time, frae him nou
cryin
in the licht.

And the flood in him.
A young God challengin
the storm rushin owre
wi him licht to me. A pillar
above the storm.

Quick he grows daurk and strong
above my heid, and
in joy
cairry him high. They turn
frae our hills in rage.
Doors are closed and shut
against the licht. Daurk doors
I canna ring. And blin.

The gairden grows wi weeds
and maggots eat the fruit. The fences
faa and wood-worms rot
the trees. The storm blaws;
and the trees
live wi fungus
and quick-footed centipedes.

Heich up hill paths I staun
and glimpse faur blue hills
and lochs seen bricht
though ne'er reached. And he
smiles owre my shouther
a rock abune the storm
I face.
She turns me to see
his weys. To journeys I canna

mak. And a stranger moves
across a field. And through
my storm. A young face.
A column broken and swept
in spate
to the sea.

The storm beats doun my airms
and the sky faas . . .

IV

Shadows grow colours
aa roun. I lie warm
in days lang wi daurk nichts
alane in their time.

A time o warmth by the fire.
Aa nicht
cauld doun daurk corridors
live wi steps
I turn frae across my nicht
and shut out
ahint quick-closed dreams.

I sit in the movin licht
wi steerin stairs
turnin wi the sparkle
o smells frae daurk breakfasts
you rise to mak
and mak again.

I sit cauld. Time
steady
in my pulse
racin to a time
I turn frae. A time o shut
doors
I couldna open
for licht or daurk.

Swallin doors growin shut
afore that white waa.
I look
to her warm in the sun. A young face
sad in my een. But quick
turn to quicker feet
and shoutin voices. Hers and mine
I canna hear, but ken

and feel aye there
a pool to lie in warm
wi unturnt licht.

My time.
But they caa
and it is Their time.

I staun against the door
and turn open-e'ed to cross
daurk corridors and shout
my strength to the shadows
that rin wi me
aye a step ahint
across haas and up stairs
to daurk that waits
and waits. And I turn warm;
turn to the fire wi them
in times unkent; daurkness
welcomed and warm
coverin us in the hidden places
o the gairden.

The leaves are faain.
I auld in their gairden;
I turn
and turn again
to a gairden that shuts out
tomorrow's licht and shadows.
I turn frae the cool watter
and desire only the saft gress
uncut since we walkt paths
seen again frae that heavy wey
across the hill;

and licht lengthens her shadow
in my dreed;
a cauld haun in mine
across corridors I see
open out
and warm carpeted.

I see her often there
an unseen face
kent across daurk gress
frae this fireside. Our past
still in me wi the toom
rooms o bairnheid. And quick
turn in warmth to her I ken
across anither field. But then

in time
grow cauld and turn
to the waa.

Sma faces growein frae petterns.
Faces safe in my een
that blink to blin
and turn
awa to ithers. Turn and turn
again. Sma movin figures
I canna ken. And lie
warm in the coloured waa
that kens nae time
but the wun movin
a leaf. A wun
aye in the gairden
and the mornin taen wi the sun . . .

and they caa
and it is their time
and their place . . .

and the advance gaes on
wi me
lyin wi you . . .

CHAPTER 18

The New Nominalism

IN A previous chapter I referred to my naming of the new (or newish)
post-romantic sesibility as a 'new nominalism'. This theory of the new
nominalism is dear to my intellectual heart but I push it down no-one's
throat. I do think, however, that it is part of a movement of developing
ideas and theories in relation to modern poetry. Many poets of serious
intention have built noble structures of theory but it may be that even
when very influential they are of greatest value to the poet who
constructed them in giving him intellectual supports for his poetry.

Like almost everyone who has written a lot I have my favourite
quotations and I would quote three here. I have long believed with
Coleridge, taking his words as a comment on life as well as on poetry:
'Beautiful is that in which the many still seen as many become one.'
And I like to think I am at least sometimes at one with Dante when he
wrote:

> Io mi son un che quando
> amor me spira, nota ed a quel modo
> che ditto deutro, vo significando
>
> (I am one who, when love breathes in me,
> take note, and that mode which he dictates
> within, go signifying)

And thirdly I agree with Wallace Stevens when he wrote: 'The theory
of poetry as the life of poetry.'

I have written oblique and impersonal essays on my theories of the
'new nominalism' but this is a personal book so here I will state these
theories in relation to my own poetry. But let me first quote a poem
from my sequence 'Of Philosophers and Tinks' from *Realities Poems*
which, as I have already said, is a sequence situated in a pub where a
group of friends are gathered. It is not John, the professional academic
philosopher, who is speaking but one of the 'Tinks', which is not of
course to suggest that a Tink cannot also be a philosopher, even if not a
professional one:

XXIII
TALE TELLER

John tell us about Nominalism
and its fecht wi Realism. Duns Scotus
splittin aa wide open in the medieval debate
and naethin the same again.

The wey prepared for William of Ockham and the end
o the Church unitin aa thocht. God nou
a Big Hie-heid Ane and to be stood afore
individual to Individual; man to God.

Tell us o the battle of Luther and the rise o black-coatit
meenisters and Scotland the only official
land o Calvinism. The impulse to Capitalism
frae the white-faced nominalist Protestants.

Aa participatin communities and ceremonial life
near deid and gone. Aa individuals,
but set apairt, and competition
aawhaur frae infant school to international strife.

Logical positivism gien its heid in philosophy
and aa nou legalistic authority in religion. And hou
the battle gaes furrit in the fecht atween
Idealism and Realism.[1]

And the poets o the new nominalism bringin in
the fluid speerit o a community o universal life
without the loss o individuality. An imaginative
union possible within a creative conflict.

A new peacfu sensibility wi the particulars
in their place but the essences in theirs. Aa
fluid and the intellect at full stretch as
lovin passion and the run o the blood.

Tell us John . . .
In your ain words . . .

In his long essay in *Akros* 33, April 1977, Alastair Mackie wrote of
me:

'Duncan Glen demands to be taken seriously. Alone, of all the
poets except MacDiarmid, he has tried to construct a platform
and provide a programme for the kind of verse he wants to write,
which is expounded in his book *The Individual and the Twentieth-*

---

[1] The medieval Realism can be equatit wi today's Idealism and the medieval Nominalism wi the modern Realism, roughly speakin.

Century Scottish Literary Tradition. Carlos Williams is his cultural father with his commitment to a speech that shall be local, i.e. rooted in an American context and thus universal. For Glen the cultural context is his Scotland, the speech his kind of Scots. Naturally this has nothing to do with a fenced parochialism: Glen's parish is not merely his Lowland locale, its marches are the expanding and contracting embrace of his consciousness. For he is particularly sensitive not only to the experience but to the 'games' as he calls them, that this open consciousness plays in the process of its thinking and feeling, its contemplation of its self in being. He probes the indeterminate zones where the "I" and the "me", the subject studying itself as object, constantly split and fuse in the flux of experience. Words therefore become the landscape where the creative ego – he doesn't approve of the word – articulates and defines itself at that moment in the poem. Glen is a modern nominalist in that he formulates his position by directly linking himself with Williams' aphorism 'no ideas but in things'. The kind of poetry he advocates, the poetry of a nominalist sensibility, is fed " . . . from a full field of modern consciousness where the poets must surely be eaducted in the fluid, graphic and electric forms *as well as* in the literal and phonetic forms". Or as he puts it else-where in his essay, " . . . the new, fluxing and mosaic-forming Electric Age as described by McLuhan".'

For a few years after the publication of my book *The Individual and the Twentieth-Century Scottish Literary Tradition* in 1971 everywhere I went I met people who had read it and who wished to discuss with me the ideas in it. This in England almost more than in Scotland. I remember the active interest in my book at the first Cambridge Poetry Festival at which I chaired a very lively forum on Scottish poetry. And twelve years after its publication young poets were still discovering it and apparently finding it useful. The young poet, W. N. Herbert, wrote to me in 1983 when he sent me his sequence 'Dundee Doldrums' which, as I have said, I printed in *Akros* 51 (October 1983) and consider, to repeat myself, to be one of the most exciting pieces of work I received in my many years of editing *Akros*. Bill Herbert said to me: 'I'm sending you this sequence of poems not in your capacity as *Akros* editor, but as a poet. I'm prompted to do this mainly by the position you set forth in *The Individual and the Twentieth-Century Scottish Literary Tradition* which crystallised for me the dilemma of a Scottish poet's Scottishness.'

Not that it has been only Scottish poets who have responded to the ideas of that book. Jeremy Hooker, in a review in *Anglo-Welsh Review* (summer 1972), wrote: 'Duncan Glen's challenging book is itself an emphatic rejoinder to the lie of The Centre. And it prompts one to ask when critics in England and Wales will wake up to what has been going on around them and help to create a culture in which centre can speak to centre instead of perpetuating the idea of a culture in which one or two centres address their far-flung peripheries. Moreover, as Duncan Glen shows so intelligently, it is in the field of new relationships, especially between the poet's language and his apprehension of reality, that we must be prepared to risk our "folly".'

It is strange, and wonderful, how a book published only in a small edition can take on a life of its own. In *The Individual . . .* I saw the poetic mainstream of our age in American/English/Scottish literature as being the open form of Whitman, Pound, Carlos Williams, the early Eliot, and the MacDiarmid of *A Drunk Man Looks at the Thistle* and the later long poems. All these poets took the step into the *individual* and free-growing forms which seem to me to most fully express our modern consciousness. Later, but still pioneering, American poets such as Charles Olson with his theories of 'projective verse' or 'composition by field' have continued this movement, as have other, even younger, American poets from Black Mountain College and elsewhere; I think of Robert Creeley and Edward Dorn, but a long list could be compiled.

Perhaps not surprisingly – he gave his blessing to Olson's theories of 'composition by field' – to Carlos Williams 'The poem is made of things – on a field'. One of the things in the 'field' in addition to other things such as a red wheelbarrow, or a rose, is words. A word has referential power but it is also one of the creative things in the field. and before putting it in the field we can take it and lift it and clean it. We can make sure it has value. Williams cried, 'No symbolism is acceptable' but it was obviously important to that wizard of the 'unadorned' word that his words had true naming power. He had none of the fear of naming experienced by the Symbolist, and even by Wallace Stevens who shows the 'romantic' dualistic tradition meeting the new 'field' tradition, or at least the nominalistic qualities of that tradition. For Stevens the poem is 'not ideas about the thing but the thing itself' as it was for Williams.

Carlos Williams most certainly achieved the symbolic value to be found only in a particular and individual cultural situation. This field theory of reality is still sometimes seen as a new idea but the theorists of language and culture have been writing about it for almost as long as the writers have been expressing it creatively. In an excellent essay 'Symbolization and Value' published as long ago as 1959 in her book *Freedom and Culture* Dorothy Lee wrote, language:

'is not a system of names for passively sensed objects and relations already existing in the outer world; but neither does it fit experience into predetermined moulds. It is a creative process, in which the individual has an agentive function; it is part of a field, which contains, in addition to the world of physical reality, the sensing and thinking individual, and the experienced reality. In this way each word, each grammatical formation, is not an empty label to be applied; it has meaning, not because meaning has been arbitrarily assigned to it, but because it contains the meaning of the concrete situations in which it participates and has participated, and which it has helped to create. With participation in situations the meaning of the symbol increases; and when the situation contains value, the symbol itself contains and conveys value.'

So the word is part of the field of reality created by the individual writer. And the poem – an object in its own reality – exists as a field of reality for each new individual reader of it. This 'field' does not exist outside the individual's personal reality as he creates his 'now' whilst reading the poem. This 'field' is to be seen expressed in many of our twentieth-century art forms from high art poetry to pop music programmes on television. This is indeed an age of flux and mosaic.

Of course the true naming of poets is as old as poetry itself and indeed the symbolic value of names is very strong in many primitive peoples' culture and perhaps can be seen as an expression of attitudes which existed in our own pre-historic ancestors. In her book mentioned above Dorothy Lee refers us to a fascinating study of the Bella Coola Indians of British Columbia by T. F. McIlwraith. The Bella Coola had a complex culture involving ceremony and gift-giving, the purpose of which was to give symbolic value to names and to specially prepared pieces of copper which, when they had been invested with the correct symbolic values, were thrown ceremoniously into the fire where their value flowed out and into the dead. The coppers were then valueless and had to go through again the long and expensive process of value-giving created by the individual in relation to communal ceremony. This, it seems to me, is not so very different from what each poet has to do for each of his poems.

It also seems to me that it is just what too many Scottish poets of the last two hundred years have failed to do. When the first white traders made contact with the Bella Coola they quickly realised that the coppers had value to the Indians. Typically, they manufactured coppers for themselves to use in trading; without success, as the coppers had true symbolic value and were worthless outside the concrete cultural situation which gave them value. For the past two hundred years or so too many Scottish poets have acted like white traders to the English literary tradition.

So I believe that we Scots have to avoid becoming writers of second-hand poetry due to cultural imperialism. But surely, also, we have to look outwards and what a delight is the international world of creative ideas. The 'composition by field' theories of Olson have been supported by a whole host of exciting ideas from a diversity of quarters and disciplines. My excitement in response to ideas leaves me open to attack as do my attempts to create art-languages in my theorising. Academics, or pseudo-academics, who do not understand the creative process or the needs of the creative writer are suspicious of such writings and tend sometimes to attack them. As Jeremy Hooker said in his review of *The Individual and the Twentieth-Century Literary Tradition:* 'inevitably, Duncan Glen takes risks in interpretating the "new sensibility", since it is by nature fluid and in motion. He writes about important seminal ideas in a way that it would be all too easy to dismiss as pretentious, and largely because he is genuinely excited by them. Few things have been more deadening to modern critical theory than embarassment in face of ideas, though this is an English rather than a Scottish failure of nerve, as the example of MacDiarmid shows. Duncan Glen's principal commitment is to Scottish poetry and his wholehearted admiration for MacDiarmid is not the least attractive feature of the book: if he has a proper sense of his own significance as a writer it is not bought at the expense of reverence for others. But he has much of importance to say about modern poetry in Europe and America.'

There are inevitably certain times in a poet's life when he is particularly open to intellectual influence but the poet who closes his mind at an early age is perhaps likely to cease being a poet; not, of course, that intellectual activity ensures continued success as a poet. But even if a poet remains open to ideas it takes time for him to articulate these ideas outside his poetry, assuming he ever wants to do this, which many do not. For myself the poetry was, I believe, written as it came and then I found theoretical supports for it. And then the poetry developed and I found new supports. And so on.

People link me, naturally enough, with MacDiarmid and, of course, the theories I put forward of being true to a native Scottish language and reality were first expounded influentially by MacDiarmid in the twenties. Not that I see all of MacDiarmid's practice as being applicable to my own poetic practice or, indeed, the practice of my generation in general. As long ago as 1971 in *The Individual and the Twentieth-Century Scottish Literary Tradition* I wrote:

'There has been a tendency for some critics, and indeed poets, to think that the very important and influential and creatively encouraging theories that MacDiarmid built up around his use of

Scots, and which have given us the wonderful Scottish renaissance movement in poetry and made it easier, or indeed possible, for us younger poets to write in Scots, have become a law which must be handed down and continued, and that all who do otherwise must fail to achieve important poetry in Scots. I think particularly of his ideas on a Joycean extension of language. Certainly the austerity of much recent European poetry, which also includes a sort of surrealism, is quite at variance with a lot of 'renaissance' theorising with regard to language. This austerity movement of Europe has affinities with current developments in American poetry, stemming from Pound and Carlos Williams.

It would be surprising if such a world-wide movement of our present times and sensibility was not also finding expression through poets writing in Scots, and that austerity movement cannot be denied because it was not anticipated in the theorising of earlier Scots-writing poets – indeed they could not be expected to anticipate it since by its very nature the *new* cannot be anticipated. Not, of course, that this "making new" is out of line with the fundamental, and creatively dynamic, theories of the renaissance movement as expounded by Hugh MacDiarmid who, when he first began to write in Scots, made it very clear that he was interested in a revival of Scots only if the word "revival" was synonymous with encouraging "the unexplored possibilities of vernacular expression". These explorations are still continuing and the best of the Scots-writing poets are continuing to work with a European rather than a provincial outlook.'

I have been described as the true disciple of MacDiarmid but I like to think that whilst acknowledging my debt I have also repaid him by learning from him that we have to 'Be yoursel'. But apart from disagreeing with him on some theoretical matters I like to think that I have developed his ideas in relation to contemporary ideas and, indeed, MacDiarmid in a letter to me dated 21st November 1971, when he had just received a copy of *The Individual* . . . wrote 'I am sure it is one of the best things you have done. That does not mean that I agree with a lot of it, but merely that I welcome it as an extension of the field of debate.' Later in the letter he wrote: 'your essays fortify the basic demands for the revival and extended application of the Scots language and bring to the task quotations and considerations from a wide range of literary and philosophical phenomena, many of which are new and as such were not available to me when I was busy indicating possible or desirable lines of development 40-50 years ago.'

Despite these acknowledgments to MacDiarmid's influence on my theorising I like also to acknowledge the non-Scottish influences on my work and theories and like to think that Ken Edward Smith was right when in his essay 'Scottish Poetry as I See It 1965-1981' in *Akros 50*

(October 1982) he saw me as having in common with Edwin Morgan: 'an openness of form and theme, a determination to link Scottishness and internationalism, and a belief that nothing is alien to the poet.' So I draw in ideas from anywhere I come across them and descend upon them as a poetic magpie and not an academic theoriser. I use the word magpie but I like to think that I pursue themes and do not just hop from this to that. Christopher Rush in his essay in *Akros* 45 (December 1980) very generously wrote of my interests as a poet: 'from a purely objective standpoint, there is little doubt that Duncan Glen remains the most ambitious of the younger makars. His canvases are larger, his intellectualism more disparate and wide-ranging, his enthusiasms carried further than those of any of his younger contemporaries. He is at once the Man of Feeling and the true disciple of Hugh MacDiarmid.'

Marshall McLuhan is now out of favour but I still believe, despite his obvious excesses, that he did a good job in bringing together important ideas out of the intellectual air of the sixties – and in developing these ideas. His pointing to the Gothic was, I believe, important. He saw it as a 'pre-Raphael or pre-Gutenberg quest for a unified mode perception' and drew our attention to Ruskin's description in *Modern Painters* (vol. 3) of a fine grotesque as, 'the expression, in a moment, by a series of symbols thrown together in bold and fearless connection, of truths which it would have taken a long time to express in any verbal way, and of which the connection is left to the beholder to work out for himself; the gaps, left or overleaped by the taste of the imagination, forming the grotesque character'. It could be a description of much modern literature, from Rimbaud's *Illuminations* or Joyce's works, to many a poem in today's magazines. With regard to Joyce, McLuhan saw him having accepted the grotesque 'as a mode of broken or syncopated manipulation to permit *inclusive* or simultaneous perception of a total and diversified field. Such, indeed, is symbolism by definition – a collection, a *parataxis* of components representing insight by carefully established ratios, but without a point of view or lineal connection or sequential order.'

This writing of McLuhan is part of the modern movement of ideas which has encouraged us to awaken once again from what Blake termed 'Newton's sleep' and the writings of Blake have influenced me as they have many another contemporary writer. I truly believe that we should use our intellects to their fullest extent but in the end the intuitive imagination is what takes us creatively forward into new areas of consciousness whether we are scientists or poets. So I believe that we poets have to defend the creative imagination from narrow and restrictive mechanistic reason. We have to avoid selling out as described in Blake's lines from *The Song of Los:*

> Thus the terrible race of Los and Enitharmon gave
> Laws and Religions to the sons of Har, binding them more
> And more to Earth, closing and restraining,
> Till a Philosophy of Five Senses was complete.
> Urizen wept and gave it into the hands of Newton and Locke.

That is an important message for poets or anyone in danger of becoming a mechanistic thinker although the English literary tradition including its critical tradition in all its width is open to us and we do not have to say that Blake is of supreme importance to us. Coleridge is just as important to me and aspects of Shelley and Keats and Arnold and so on. My interest in older and newer literary criticism can be seen in a long essay I wrote for *Akros* 37 (April 1978) under the title 'Of Poetries and Pigs' and the pseudonymn Robert Brooks. But for all my interest in literary criticism I quote from William's *Paterson* in the above-mentioned essay:

> The province of the poem is the world,
> when the sun rises, it rises on the poem
> and when it sets darkness comes down
> and the poem is dark

So in the end we turn not to criticism but to poems. Again I do not have to choose who is of most importance to me as the whole of English language poetry is directly available to me but probably Wordsworth is the pre-twentieth century English language poet who speaks most directly to me the most often. Some critics have suggested that I was influenced by *The Prelude* when I wrote *In Appearances* but I have shamefully to confess that I had not read Wordsworth's masterpiece when I wrote my book. The writings of Wordsworth are, however, responded to in 'Follow! Follow! Follow!' in *Realities Poems* although his sense of God from nature is not a vision I can accept uncritically, having lived intellectually through a 'God is dead' silence and reached a non-dogmatic sense of the single creative One – of God if you like; as I wrote at the end of 'Follow! Follow! Follow!' with a reference to Wordsworth in the first line which I quote:

> A motion and a spirit indeed
> but new within a singleness that taks in
> the broken Roman windaes
> as the Sistine Chapel and the goal achieved for itsel.
> The breath drawn for the cry o the moment
> and leid wi it. This being in petterned moments
> out o the air . . .

the tall lums o Clydeside steelwarks
the movin hymns to a yirdit God heard frae the street
the daurk heicht o the Cuillins
the ordered warld o Dante entered into
the flowin Clyde fouled by technology seen blue again
the immanence o Him naiturally taen by Wordsworth seen wi oursel
the drivin watters o Burniebrae seen movin thegither
the God o Abraham and Isaac taen for Himsel

And them at Parkheid and Ibrox wi a new voice.

Aa that is in being
stauns real
and clear o the newest daurk. Aa
rax out to be wi the realness o things for themsels
that can mak a glow as warm as luve o anither
taen without a thocht o sel.

Follow! Follow! Follow!

As Alastair Mackie said, I am interested in the 'games' that the mind plays and as a poet I am, of course, interested in language games, which brings to mind Ludwig Wittgenstein and for me also his philosophical successors who remind us that our stance in the landscape of reality is dependent upon syntax. Wittgenstein's ideas pop up quite often in my poetry although usually by indirect means, although his direct influence can be seen in some poems including 'Words' from *In Appearances* which it pleased me to have Robert Garioch include in his anthology *Made in Scotland* as this is a poem I like but which has been ignored by critics of my work.

WORDS

We can sclim up by words
and seein the nonsense
play anither gemm. We hae broken
out o boxes
and gae up and doun.
Ae gemm efter the ither.

I'm a Scot and can play wi Calvin
for a while ony day.
We hae Sanctification by the Spirit
frae Justification by the Faith.
There's words for you. There's aye
Free Will and Predestination thegither.
I can mind my Catechism
word by word.

Words gaein back and back. I ken the weys
afore my time. Nae pentit ornaments
or kist o whistles. Psalms set aff
by the Precentor rinnin up the scale.
And the tunes. 'Colehill', 'French'
and bonny 'Martyrdom' lullin Scottish bairns
to sleep mony a nicht.
I ken them aa.

We kent richt frae wrang aa spellt out.
We could sing psalms sittin doun
and hae lang prayers staunin up
said richt frae the hert.
We can argue wi God oursels
– mindin our Catechism and gien proofs.
We hae the word.

Times hae changed.
There's nae caain to cutty stool
for us. Nae up afore the Kirk Session.
I'm o my day.

Here's nae lust for beauty
or the settin up o Airt. Nae ceremony
o sound or licht is needit here.
Nat pentit idols. We hae the Word
and ken what's richt frae wrang.

Calvin the man o God
– and law and logic.
And us his people
wi our past.

But I ken Wittgenstein nou
and I hae my gemms.

Another influential writer of my first days as a writer of critical theory was Claude Lévi-Strauss. He made it academically and 'poetically' known that physical science had to discover that a 'semantic universe possesses all the characteristics of an object in its own right for it to be recognised that the manner in which primitive peoples conceptualise their world is not merely coherent but the very one demanded in the case of an object whose elementary structure presents the picture of a discontinuous complexity'.

And we have had Lévi-Strauss further arguing most convincingly, in *The Savage Mind*, that it is:

'scientific *praxis* which, among ourselves, has emptied the notions of death and birth of everything not corresponding to mere physiological processes and rendered them unsuitable to convey other meanings. In societies with initiation rites, birth and death provide the material for a rich and varied conceptualisation, provided that these notions (like so many others) have not been stripped by any form of scientific knowledge orientated towards practical returns – which they lack – of the major part of a meaning which transcends the distinction between the real and the imaginary: a complete meaning of which we can now hardly do more than evoke the ghost in the reduced setting of figurative language. What looks to us like being embedded in *praxis* is the mark of thought which genuinely takes the words it uses seriously, whereas in comparable circumstances we only "play" on words.'

No doubt in most everyday circumstances the modern western mind does indeed only 'play' on words, but there are *other* circumstances – poetic circumstances. Also it is my belief that with our developing post-romantic consciousness – with what I call the 'new nominalism' – we stand at a crossroads comparable to that at which the western mind stood when John Donne wrote his famous lines on the new philosophy although our new response to reality is as much a psychological and mental one of the imagination as a 'practical' scientific one and I do not underestimate the re-orientation of our minds which has been caused by the development of technology and science, not least the communication technologies on which McLuhan was so good. We are a long way from seeing how the electronic media will affect the printed word but already we can see reference material switching to electronic storage. How long can the British telephone directory last in printed form? All this is in the immediate future and what will happen in twenty or fifty years is beyond anyone's forecast. But beyond question the electronic systems are going to further change how we see our stance in what I have already called the landscape of reality.

Having referred to John Donne's famous lines I must quote them even although they have become over-used:

> And new philosophy calls all in doubt:
> The element of fire is quite put out;

The road founded in the seventeenth century led past Galileo to Descartes and to Hobbes – to mechanistic and scientific rationalism. The road we seem now to be taking appears superficially to go beyond Descartes in materialism. MacDiarmid commands:

> Do not argue with me. Argue with these stones.
> Truth has no trouble in knowing itself.
> This is it. The hard fact. The inoppugnable reality.

And Wallace Stevens wishes the poem to be:

> ...the cry of its occasion,
> Part of the res itself and not about it.

But it is a materialism which takes in 'A view of New Haven, say, through the certain eye' of Stevens; and in which:

> We seek
> Nothing beyond reality. Within it,
>
> Everything, the spirit's alchemicana
> Included, the spirit that goes roundabout
> And through included, not merely the visible.
>
> The solid, but the movable, the moment,
> The coming on of feasts and the habits of saints,
> The pattern of the heavens and high, night air.

It is a wonderful, rich, human inheritance and as Williams, at the beginning of *Paterson*, commands: 'Say it, no ideas but in things' and at the end of *Paterson Three* cries:

> Let
> me out! (well, go!) this rhetoric
> is real!

As I have said in my Introduction to *The Akros Anthology of Scottish Poetry 1965-70*, already quoted from, this new road or new sensibility of the past-romantic, modern western nominalist mind is not yet easily expressible in prose and indeed one of its qualities is its very unexpressiveness – the difficulty of seeing it in a fixed stance since one of its qualities is that of continual flux and change. It is of it that Wallace Stevens, who perhaps only truly broke into an acceptance of the new nominalist sensibility in his later work, wrote when he described, in lines I have already quoted, 'the giant of nothingness, each one/And the giant everchanging, living in change'. And yet despite both the 'nothingness' and the ever-changing quality of this new sensibility it is also of it that Marianne Moore wrote when, after Yeats on Blake if I remember right, she referred to 'literalists of the imagination' and cried for a poetry in which real toads can be set in an imaginary garden. Certainly I personally have found no imaginative difficulty in accepting such realities and indeed I believe that I had taken them for granted long before I knew the theories, as my poetry can perhaps prove to anyone who approaches it imaginatively (another paradox) as a 'literalist of the imagination' and who can accept that the world exists as it is for each of us in our own realities which, once accepted, are surprisingly real to all those who can accept them in their ever-changing concreteness which appears as the reverse of concrete to those who can accept neither the fact of living in change nor the 'nothingness' which we enter into and from which we draw our reality, including language which we create in action – on the rhythmic move – through poetry.

I have referred to our nominalism as modern, but I was careful to qualify it as the modern *western* mind to which I was referring and perhaps it is only a discovery – or rather a re-discovery since we have had the Bible for a long time – in the west of what eastern thinking has long recognised; a return to a dogmaless 'religious' way of thinking. It is not for nothing that for quite a long time now so many young people have been looking east to find parallels with attitudes they seem to find within themselves. Of course Yeats was there before it became a 'pop' way of life and a popular or underground movement in poetry, al-though the simplicist stream of consciousness movement associated with this movement is only one expression of our rediscovery of the essential Oneness of ourselves in movement. This energy force,· or movement, or field is apparently many-sided and yet it is truly *real* only in the united fluidity of our Now or our Oneness from which we 'start' and which, it seems, can be 'known' only in movement – or through its manifestations; manifestations of self to self or self to non-self by which we can know ourselves but which are not a self but a manifesta-tion of self. We can see the result or the movement can seem to stop them through language to give us our moments or seemingly fixed nows although, as the Tantric theorists can tell us so well, the language in turn is simply an action to create something new which can lead to the true rest of our Oneness (with the cosmos, or with the imagination or with God if you prefer that imagery). Our apparent stoppings or moments are really other ceremonies and other movements and another aspect of the One or the Now of our One; this without it being the Now or indeed it being ourselves. As Moses saw in his revelation of God, ' "I AM THAT I AM I AM," ' . . . Thus shalt thou say . . . I AM hath sent me unto you.' And in Brahmin metaphysics, as I take them as. a poet, we have the same principles beautifully worked out (the Siva and Sakti for example) and we can know that the united self steps out of itself to be aware of itself and so creates a subject with its object the 'reality' in which the object is truly the subject or the One. According to Tantra the ultimate reality is the Union of Siva and Sakti, which is the pure consciousness which looks on or is static united with the active or kinetic aspects or energy of the universe. The sexual aspects of Tantric mysticism which interested Yeats come to mind here, but Tantric thinking can, it seems, take in modern atomic theory as it can also take in the time-space continuum. But the strongest image, for me, of this wonderful resolution of the apparent dual aspect of man and the universe and of the opposing two seen as the essential one is the Upanishad image of the two birds: 'two birds, inseparable companions, cling to the self-same tree. Of these one eats the sweet fruit, the other looks on without eating.' Here, I believe, we are at the core of creation and at the threshold of an understanding of the 'new' non-lineal and non-'materialistic' consciousness now being expressed, once again, in western literature. So what we require, I believe, is not to see ourselves on a road which has passed Einstein and which goes from Here to There or from a Cartesian I and You to an Egoless One, but rather as being on a central static roundabout (in a time-space continuum if you like); a circular island on which – to quote again from *Paterson* – 'anywhere is everywhere' and upon which the modern mind enacts its 'magic' ceremony:

> We know nothing and can know nothing
> but
> the dance, to dance to a measure
> contrapuntally,
> Satyrically, the tragic foot.

One of the essentials of these open forms of poetry, as indeed it may be of any form of poetry, is that the poet is true to his own local roots including, surely, a literary language created from the speech he heard around him from birth. MacDiarmid fought a battle for a literary language native to him. And so, indeed, did Carlos Williams and Charles Olson with their theories of an individual breath-and-speech measure.

Every poet struggling towards his identity has to build anew, even if on the base of a tradition, but he must do it, surely, without compromise. As MacDiarmid said:

> I'll ha'e nae hauf-way hoose, but aye be whaur
> Extremes meet – it's the only way I ken
> To dodge the curst conceit o' bein richt
> That damns the vast majority o' men.

I'll bury nae heid like an ostrich's
Nor yet believe my een and naething else
My senses may advise me, but I'll be
Mysel' nae maitter what they tell's . . .

Not, as Alastair Mackie said, that I approve of ego trips for poets. This being true to oneself is a self-less idea; if a poet thinks of his own 'image', of the impression he is making to the world, he will surely fail as a poet even if he temporarily succeeds as a literary politician. But just as Williams fought for an American idiom true to himself so must we, surely, search for our own true-to-our-own-realities idiom. It would be sad, just when the Americans have perhaps thrown off the falsifying effects of Europe on their poetry if our realities were falsified by Americanisation. This is not a plea for European or Scottish isolationism. As will already be obvious, I believe we require all the knowledge that we can get of what the world is doing; we require all the craft and cleverness at our disposal but without each being 'ourself' we can surely only fail. Finally, for all the craft or skill in the world, the poet has to have the courage to grow with the poem – Keat's 'negative capability' if you like. It is one of the things that sorts out the poets from those who have learned a few skills and linguistic tricks. It is essential to the success of the 'open field' theories of Olson's 'projective verse' and very much a part of the nominalist's acceptance of 'the now'. To do this, although the poet will reject the ego, he has to be fully true to himself – to his individual reality or 'now' – in the poem. Of course, this can lead not to an egoless yet individual poetic self but to vatic *self*-conscious, personal, private posturings that have filled so many poetry magazines and not a few pages of anthologies. But such poetic failures do not by themselves invalidate such poetic theories – they only prove the failure of some poets, although the apparent lack of the need for 'learned' skills obviously leads to more people attempting poetry and so to many more non-poems. Although who is to say what can come out of this great upsurge in poetry-writing.

But what many of these poets lack is not only technique (academically or intuitively known) but the ability for the intellectual activity – the construction (which is also an intuitional seizing!) of an Idea which can encompass a co-ordinated view of life or reality and which the poet 'knows' whole and yet has to strive towards in the poetry, and which provides the mind with the supports that enable the imagination to flourish and create the 'new'. Intellectuals who build up philosophical structures for themselves without the intuitional 'seizing' behind them are, of course, as ill-equipped for poetry as the anti-intellectual egoists interested only in 'self-expression'. Carlos Williams had his 'American

Idea' as MacDiarmid had his 'Scottish Idea' which had several names, and Yeats had his 'Ireland Idea'. It also seems, for all that I believe with Carlos Williams that 'the past is for those that lived in the past', that to live successfully as a poet in the 'now', poets need a tradition and a culture created by 'their' society – their cultural entity – to support them and to kick off from into their own reality – the Now – created by the imagination.

Cover of The Akros Anthology of Scottish Poetry 1965-70 designed by Duncan Glen and published in 1970.

Cover of Akros 50, October 1982, designed by George Hollingworth.

CHAPTER 19

There and Now

THE POETIC theories I have written about are, as I have stressed, prose or intellectual supports for my own poetry, but the poetic expression on which these theories are based is to be found throughout my work. Here I would quote, as example, the final poem of the sequence 'Ane to Anither' from *Realities*. It is entitled simply 'There':

A tall girl.
I see her daurk agin the sky
heich on the banks o the hillside loch.

There's a solitary tree to her left equally daurk
and a stane dyke rinnin up to the richt.
A burn's feedin into the loch
owre chuckie stanes and wee dam
wi soothin sounds.

Nou I see me by her side
and deuks are takin aff
heich owre the heid o a solitary fisherman
faur owre the loch.

As aye it is you my luve.
You say nae word and mak nae movement
o heid or haund or ee
but aa is open communication frae you
to me.

I sit in the warmth o your communion
ayont this or ony leid.

But thae words are there tae in the movement
wi loch and tree
stane dyke and feedin burn. Wi
you and I
and my thochts. Words
I lift out o the silent moment
for this new structure
individual to itsel as thae objects
I name
yet made anew time and again as needit
unique to the moment.

I see mysel that solitary fisherman
but sixteen
castin out owre the loch time and time again
lang afore I kent you
a pairt o the naitural scene it seems.
The quait lappin o the loch agin the bank
and the stillin o the wund wi the settin sun
as if a speerit movin through the gloamin licht
and yet the sun there
hauf a sphere bricht orange to the West.

And nou you and I thegither in this scene
without touchin or brakin the sherp silence
owre and ayont the burn rinnin owre the chuckies
and the dam
into the depths o the loch.

And that fisherman fishin on.

I see you daurk agin the sky
as that young fisherman
and me by your side
at peace. And yet this moment
dynamic being
– a stream and a counter-stream.

Aa is kent for itsel
in the movements o this leid
definin and creatin . . .

the burn, the single tree, the stane dyke
you and me, thae words. An essence
in aa things
there in intimations and sensed in intuitions
– and hesitate to name . . .

though there in this moment . . .

The Logos?
And become flesh through a luve
ayont unnerstaunin?

I turn to you clear agin the sky . . .

CHAPTER 20

Arrivals and Departures

D ETAILS of moves from place to place by my wife and myself are given strictly accurately in my long poem *On Midsummer Evenin Merriest of Nichts?* which is mostly as fluid with regard to time and situation, and indeed as liable to poetic licence with seeming autobiography, as are most (or all) of my poems. I often base a poem, or a section of a poem, on some experience of my life but for creative reasons usually take poetic licence with it in large or small measure. Sometimes, of course, incidents which read like autobiography are entirely the product of my imagination. But the following is, indeed, in accurate 'chronological dimension':

> I hear your voice for real, but private to me,
> as I see our traivels thegither in chronological dimension –
> Fife to Houghton to Godmanchester to London
> to Hemel Hempstead to Glasgow
> to Preston to here in two houses
> in Radcliffe. Victorian Albert House we've left ahint.
> And nou this gairden o delicht
> here and aawhaur, ayont ony sel o you or me.

I have already described our situation in Houghton and Godman-chester. In London we had a bed-sitting room and a kitchen in a run-down but once-fine house in Eton Road, off Haverstock Hill. We decorated and generally did up our rooms much to the pleasure of our landlady, Mrs Rose. I have described the house reasonably accurately in another verse of my poem 'Houses':

V

> There are people livin in my houses.
> I hae a key to the door as hauf-a-dozen ithers.
> It's a London House. The street is leased by Eton College.
> Aince a desirable property, nou it has a movin
> population. A woman o doubtful employment
> on the ground floor and a policeman on the second
> to show aa are taen as equals if the rent is paid.
> The chairs hae been touched by scores o backsides

and the bath by hunners. A German or an Anglo-Indian
sits in my airmchair and the landlady maun be deid.
I dout if the tenants ken ony difference in her successor.
Here aa is cheynge and yet I hear the cry o bairns
livin in their first house if maistly till somewhaur better
is found. I hear the cry o a new-born bairn
and a young mither worrit about them next door
and me a faither o that house.

Eton Road is quite near to Hampstead Heath and very near to
Primrose Hill and Regent's Park and we walked often in all these green
areas. I used images from Regent's Park and Primrose Hill in 'John
Atman' from *In Appearances*, which I have already quoted, although
in the poem the geography has probably become Scottish; but it was
London and Regent's Park I had in my mind's eye when I wrote:

She walks pink and cool
doun stairs and through doors,
dress swingin owre uneven
streets; across green paths,
and small blue ponds wi dookin birds
bricht wi greens and blues;
bricht mallards and dull ducks
paddlin ablow a pentit bridge
railed wi smooth worn planks.

And Primrose Hill was in my sights when I wrote:

And run. And run.
And run and climb that hill
high owre grey tours and hingin
reek. Saintly churches but
lines
against the sky and learnit
spires a pettern raisin us
thegither against the nicht.

In the next verse I personally see us visiting Scottish relatives and in the
following one we await the birth of a child and our first child, Ian, was
in fact born whilst we were living at Eton Road, as the verse from
'Houses' suggested. He was born in a nursing home on the edge of
Hampstead Heath. Fifteen years later I wrote a poem addressed to Ian
and it forms part of 'Days and Places' in *Realities Poems:*

IV

ARRIVALS
(To Ian)

I

I can mind the day you were born
fifteen Octobers away.

It was warm as August but daurk outside
as in the haawey wi a 40-watt bulb.

There's a stairwey leads daurkly to the ward
whaur you are being born.

I'm advised to tak a walk.
It seems you are in nae hurry.

I tak to an unpethed pairt o the Heath to be alane.
Ithers hae the same idea if in couples.

You keep me waitin the hail lang nicht
and get me up early the next mornin but waitin till the efternoon.

You are announced I presume wi a skelp
and your first cry as is traditional.

I return to a nou sunlicht haa as I mind it
and a stairwey I sclim wi lichtsome steps.

I see your mither.
Wi white coat and mask I peer doun at you.

You say nae word and dinna e'en blink an ee.
Proud, I swallow it and try to look as if

it's a naitural occurrence
to hae a first-born son.

II

Nou you are fifteen and your turn to be
proud. You find it haurd to swallow it.

You think you ken it aa
as me afore you wi my faither.

I see my younger sel staunin dour afore a question
you dinna want to accept faur less answer.

A recognition haurd to hae
wi an 'our auld bairn for aa the joy and pride.

Soon you will learn to tak us for granted again
or mebbe for oursels, adult beings

as you, soon, yoursel. A joyfu, welcome arrival
nou as then.

Also in *Realities Poems*, in the 'A Sort of Renewal' section, is a
poem which many people find moving:

XXI

TWELVE NOON

It's noon on midsimmer's day
and I think of the perfect circle.
I think of you my luve. I see you a girl
wi swayin hips. I see you bent
pickin daisies and buttercups
the slopin pasture framin you in perfect
composition. I see you lie curled on your side
aneath a great aik in simmer
and sun straught owreheid. I see you
move round in the dance
and feel your warm closeness.
I see you walk up your path
haein said guid nicht
wi the full moon heich owre your heid.
I see you bent into winter wund straught
across stubble field. I see you frae ahint
caught in a shower in simmer dress.
I see you bendin to wash dishes,
pick strawberries in our first gairden,
or a pin on the floor.
I see you bent owre a cot
to lift our son but twa weeks auld.

By the time Ian was born I had started lecturing in typographic
design at Watford College of Technology and soon we were able to
move into a flat in Hemel Hempstead at, to be precise, 11a Melsted
Road which is the address printed in MacDiarmid's pamphlet *Poetry
Like the Hawthorn*.

Our next move, from Hemel Hempstead, was to a house in Rannoch
Avenue, Bishopbriggs, Glasgow, an address which also features in
MacDiarmid pamphlets, and both Ian and the avenue we lived in,
although somewhat changed, feature in a section of *On Midsummer
Evenin Merriest of Nichts?*:

A return to Glasgow wi three-year-auld son . . .

Home from work this first day. I walk

into my new home's street. An avenue
of suburbia. Late Spring and the song of young thrushes
with wide-open throats. On the pavement
fresh green oak bent over and perfectly placed
as the road opens out to blue sky
broken by the separate whitenesses of passing clouds.

But child suddenly there on tiny tricycle
with fat bulbous wheels. His quick-moving legs
strive to be up and doun even faster
in welcoming speed. My knowing joy instincts towards
words
but silence peaks into a smile
– and I ruffle his hair.

And again nou.

As I have said, my job in Glasgow was as editor and designer with a
firm of educational publishers but I did not settle although even what
upset me most about the job resulted in a poem later:

TRUST TO GOD
(to all authoritarians)

you thocht
you were God

be on time
hae your pen
poised to scrieve
at nine o'clock

you thocht
I'd jump

as you pressed
the button

ding dong bell

you sat as God

and I sat

and did
naething

ding dong knell

you pressed the button

I got anither
job

he thocht he was God

be on time . . .

In fact I worked quite hard. My next job was not in the least one with an authoritarian boss although I have, since my Glasgow experiences, been perhaps over-ready to stand up for myself against my bosses which may be why I have ended up as something of a minor boss myself. I have a suspicion, however, that our culture pushes hard, rather unimaginative men to the very top jobs of our society. But in a section in *On Midsummer Evenin, Merriest of Nichts?*, immediately after the section on the nightmare that can be National Service, I wrote:

And civilian pintin finger?

The croud kens best, still, for pouer.
It pushes the haurdmen to the tap
and hauds them there wi its single fist.
We push against these tap dugs
and bend back as we must to survive
the croud.
Again we push and bend again
or snap. Or crawl awa
and dae what we hae to
for the sel, agin the haurd anes,
bendin and pushin
and pushin

until we can bend nae mair.

But poets are among the lucky ones, given mental stability and at least some humour to save them from their searchings into reality. My poem continues with questions and then a little song.

And me at wark safe in my Imagination
in this gairden of my delicht
and dule? Poet
safe at wark facin only mysel?
A protectit bird
in full sang or fleein heich?

'Pass the word
I'm a protectit bird.
They're settin girns for vermin
Like stoats and their kin,

The fox is huntit and shot doun
And aa to keep me safe and soun.
Pass the word
I'm a protectit bird.
You micht say august
and that is surely just.
Aa is for my health
And a pairty on the twelfth!'

And there is a tendency for almost everyone to join in that party. The next three lines of my poem read:

Aye the hunters are out in the hill
for them fleein heich
in seemin folly.

Whenever I use that word 'folly' in relation to poets (and I most sincerely believe that they have to risk 'seemin folly') I think of Hart Crane who used the word before me and whose risk-taking ended in the disaster of his suicide. I have addressed a poem to him in my long poem *The State of Scotland* and end this chapter with it as a tribute to him and as a warning that writers of poetry do indeed take risks if they are worthy of the name 'poet'.

The date is 27th April 1932
and the time a few minutes before noon.
The ship named *Orizaba*
is some three hundred miles
north of Havana.

I think of your
'Leaf after autumnal leaf
break off,
descend –
descend –'

I think of you advisin the risk of folly
in the conquest of consciousness.

You walk to the stern of the *Orizaba*
take off your coat
and step overboard
silently . . .

I see these autumn leaves falling again.
I see your coat lying still a black shape
on that polished deck

CHAPTER 21

'The Hert of Scotland'

SINCE I left Glasgow in 1965 to live in Penwortham and work in Preston I have never spent more than a fortnight in Scotland at any one time. There is a danger in a writer being an exile, but I need only mention James Joyce to show that it need not be a disadvantage to all writers. But I believe I do know my Scotland, if not *all* Scotland as indeed I humorously suggested in a poem 'The Hert of Scotland'. I do not really *know* the Highlands although in fact I do know some of the *places* I name better than I admit to in the poem. For example, I have stood in the top of Ben Nevis on a beautifully clear day when I felt I could see almost all of Scotland at my feet. I will now quote the poem, with the comment that it will never be more funny than when it was read by the late Bryden Murdoch on BBC Radio. I confess to being unable to give a reading that brings out the full humour of the poem in the way that fine actor did.

> I hae problems.
>
> I would scrieve o Scotland
> and mak a unity o it
>
> but
> ken nae word o Gaelic
> though I've had three fortnichts in the heilants
> and went on a boat to Lochboisdale
> wi hauf an 'our ashore. In Inverness I was that lanely
> I went to bed early. In Fort William it rained
> and though I sclimed Ben Nevis in record time
> it was sae misty I could haurdly see the peth at my feet.
>
> Dundee I hae forgotten frae an efternoon visit
> and Union Street, Aberdeen I've never seen to forget.
> Perth I reached efter a lang bike ride
> and had to turn back as soon as I got there
> haein nae lichts.
> Stirling Castle I hae stood on and surveyed the scene
> but I mind the girl mair than the panorama.
> The Borders I ken weill, enterin or leavin, by a sign
> SCOTLAND
> but I've never got aff the train.

I hae problems.

Fife nou is different.
It I ken frae pushin an auld bike to the limits
and stood on baith Lomonds and Largo Law: I hae kent it
early and late wi the extremes o youth. And mony
girls
but aa the faces and names nou forgotten
but ane that counts
in or out o Fife and she was born in Mallaig
whaur I'd never been.
Fife is different.
I hae my Glesca voice and Fifers notice that.
And I've never played golf at St Andrews.

I hae problems.

Still there's Edinburgh
and that gies a bit o status if no unity
for aa that aabody kens Edinburgh
(they'd hae us believe!)
I had the advantage o digs in Marchmont
and days at the Art College
– but aye a visitor wi a time limit
as still
wi sae mony ithers.

I hae problems
being frae Lanarkshire.

It's true there's the hills by Symington
and orchards in the upper Clyde valley
and Kirkfieldbank. But
I was ane that ne'er went to see the Spring blossom
steyin put in grey streets
in the shadow o pits and bings and steelwarks.
The ugliest stretch in aa Scotland
those that ken their Scotland hae tellt us
and I only kent about as faur as I could walk.

I hae problems.

There's my Scotland. A wee corner o Lanarkshire
and Glesca (I should mention!)
whaur as message boy
at fifteen I kent aa the addresses
and short cuts. There I belanged
– till I left at echteen!

CHAPTER 22

A Knitted Claymore?

WHEN *The Akros Anthology of Scottish Poetry 1965-70* was published, a *Times* critic described my Introduction, which I have already written about, as a fine piece of critical invective. A piece of vituperative writing which was more famous for a time appeared only a little later as the complete contents of the Scottish magazine *Lines Review*, No. 37, June 1971. It was 'The Knitted Claymore. An Essay on Culture and Nationalism' by Alan Jackson. This aroused a lot of interest and controversy at the time; replies to it appeared in magazines, Scottish radio gave over a programme to a discussion on it, I was interviewed by a *Guardian* reporter, but I refused to respond in kind to Jackson's vituperation and the printed fruits of the interview were only a few sentences.

Jackson's piece was essentially an anti-nationalist essay. In a letter to *The Scotsman* Jackson explained that he wrote it because he was 'disturbed by the publications and statements of a small number of Scottish writers over the last few years. They claim to be the proud bearers of a fine tradition but seem to me increasingly to display narrowness, reaction, loss of integrity and corruption of values.' He further suggested that 'the nationalism of these writers had so rigidly defined their reality that they produced intolerant, one-sided judgments and propagandist, shallow works'.

In his actual essay Jackson saw the upsurge of Scottish nationalists resulting in 'men I thought had slunk away to prickly sulks on couches of thistles or even to realise which decade of which century they lived in, came breengin' hurriedly back, reknitting their half unravelled claymores and pulling behind them pramfuls of young poets waving tartan rattles'.

Good stuff, but unfair when he goes on to quote short extracts from works by Donald Campbell, Hugh MacDiarmid, John Herdman, David Morrison, Carrubers Close (from *Akros* 10) and Tom Scott, which distort the writers' original meanings. A little later he turns to me: 'Duncan Glen, as editor of *Akros*, has always struck me as a man leaning backwards to be fair. That may be the trouble – that he has to fight a strong tendency in the opposite direction (in a way this makes it a greater achievement)'. After this flow of the imagination he then goes on to misquote me on the need for a developed Scottish language which will help to give the Scot cultural confidence. But no matter, I suppose the joy is in the vituperation which is soon forgotten. After another selection of short quotes, including two from my writings, Jackson continues: 'Gee whizzles. Sweet Jesus. Fanny my aunt, speak. Medieval forsooth. Muddy evil, for-God-saken. Is this the twentieth century or am I out of it. A void did you say? Did someone mention rubbish? No wonder the cerebellum sometimes aches. For Christ's sake, Jimmy, unclip me a song, quick. And was He living in Edinburgh all this time?'

Good fun but less good is his suggestion that given independence for Scotland these writers might be spelling it out 'in rubber truncheons'. And mild old me is forever going on 'endlessly about the English-writing Scots poets writing to "please London editors and publishers" ' and he says I give myself away when I talk, 'of the unhealthiness of a *London* acceptance compared to an *Edinburgh* one. So he does admit that there are centres, capitals, places where more things happen than some others in certain respects. If one wants acceptance (and why not; if it's fairly won?), what's up with a review in the *Sunday Times* when it will be read by twenty times more people than one in *The Scotsman*? Why not a London publisher when, *the way things are*, he is likely to have more resources and better distribution. These lads are border mad.'

I have spent slightly more years of my life in England than in Scotland and I am not for supressing any expansion of human consciousness, whether it originates from Oxbridge or Liverpool, Cardiff or Cambuslang, New York or wherever. What I have spoken up for is the freedom for these areas, and all areas, to develop without cultural suppression by economically or politically powerful forces. So I do believe, despite Alan Jackson's entertaining lecturing of me, that for centuries we Scots have been telling ourselves – and believing our own tale – that our culture is dying and Scotland the nation moving towards a final assimilation into English Anglo-Saxondom. With the recent upsurge of cultural independence this tale is less easy to put over, but it is an old tale well established even in these more enlightened days.

Each time a work of art is destroyed by war or by accident we have the righteous rising from their padded pews in righteous (and proper) horror and rage. We have a surplus of Art moralists; but why are they not rising to protest at the possible destruction of one of the cultural assets of Europe – the destruction of Scottish culture. True, the destruction is by slow and sly means but they are power-orientated means for all their sleekit ways. The main reason why there is no protest movement is that the destruction of Scotland is acquiesced in by the Scots themselves bogged down in their jammy bog of sensible-ness. If these Scots were Poles or Czechs no doubt we would right-eously call them compromisers – quislings and betrayers of their own freedom. We all know that sameness leads to half-wittedness and to sterility; we know variety is life itself. We know that is what the multitudinous richness of Art is about. It is also the reason for the Scottish literary revival of this century. But looking at sensible com-promisers keeping up with the English Jonses, or the American Lowells, and adapting and adjusting to meet the practical situations of a Scotland ruled politically and economically from London, it seems that everything in modern Scotland goes back to economic power – in the short term. In the long term (culturally) it is different; the compro-misers of the Scottish literary world lose their power – they are lost under the mass of true English or American culture – and the deep-rooted MacDiarmids and Burnses come into their own as the voice of their culture and their time.

Here again I would write of the need to defend Scots as part of the native Scottish culture, but I am not suggesting that those truly brought up to speak Scottish English should compromise themselves by writing in Scots. All-round tolerance is what I am asking for. Edwin Muir's famous and much-quoted statement to forget Scots and attempt to be absorbed into the English tradition was a potential limitation of a lot of would-be poets. So I argue for a better attitude to Scots throughout all levels of Scottish society. The cultural quislings have to be opposed as they limit our opportunities and our freedom to be ourselves in these creative acts. Alan Jackson is equally right to oppose any nationalists or anyone else who would limit freedom. But obviously attack is not enough and we have to work to build and to achieve a Scottish culture which supports those who creatively contribute to it.

There has been in recent years a welcome emergence of new inde-pendent Scottish publishers who are professional in approach yet willing to take financial risks for the sake of making creative writing available. I think of Canongate, Paul Harris Publishing, Gordon Wright, Ramsay Head Press and the recently extended work of Macdonald. But life is never easy for a new and unknown poet. Personally I am most worried about the new young Scots-writing poets not being published as they should be. There tend to be more openings for English-writing poets although in fact the sales record of books of poetry in Scots published by Akros Publications shows that there is a demand for such works. I do not push Scots writing for nationalistic reasons but simply because it just happens to be a fact that some form of Scots remains the mother tongue of the masses of Lowland Scots and therefore it follows that if all had equal opportunities it would be the dominant social literary language of Scotland. This is not my opinion alone; it is the opinion of all people who truly know about the speech of the Scottish people. As Tom McArthur, the lexicographer and linguist said: 'There are really three different languages. There is standard English, mixed Scots and full Scots. Most Scots speak the middle form. It is difficult to find a Scot who genuinely talks in full Scots.'

Interestingly, Tom McArthur also stated:

'There has certainly been a genteel literary element in the preservation of older forms but there is a tendency to forget that Scots has never faded – it's the playground language of the kids in most parts of Scotland. The language of Burns is still used spontaneously and Scots as a language of the people is not in any danger. But it does need to be better understood by academics, it also needs more elbow-room and more respect from the establishment.'

Some middle-class voices will say otherwise to Scots being the majority language of Lowland Scots, but they are seeing only the tip of the Scottish language situation – an influential, powerful and educated (and educating) tip but still only a tip. And we have to be careful about accepting unresearched opinions about modern Scots dialects. There is no properly researched evidence that regional dialects are moving towards a standardisation. It may be expected by so-called practical realists, but no-one really knows until the research has been done. There has been plenty of research into old rural Scots. The vocabulary of this rural Scots is certainly not being used by younger people in the way that it was by my maternal grandfather or my mother or even me. Changed social circumstances as much as anything are killing off the old rural Scots of my grandfather. Now there are those, usually older people, who wish to see this older Scots preserved and re-established. They believe it is the 'genuine' or 'true' or 'educated' Scots. This is nonsense. If Scots was still today, with regard to vocabulary and syntactic rules, exactly as it was in the youth or childhood of today's older people, then it would be a dead language. Living languages are always changing with regard to both vocabulary and syntactic rules. This I believe Scots is still doing, although we need research to know how extensive it is. Scots may have, under the pressures of English, changed too much in the recent past, but it still lives in a new form. It is that new Scots that makes me optimistic with regard to the future of the language. There are new words coming into urban Scots all the time as they are needed for new objects and new concepts. Research projects like the Linguistic Survey of Scotland do not reveal this new vocabulary as they are concerned with the older rural-based

Scots speakers. These new urban words are genuine Scots words and not part of Scottish-English. They are used only in regions of Scotland although some may creep into usage in the North of England. So they are part of the Scots lexicon and part of modern Scots dialects – usually urban dialects. And as part of regional dialects they will be known and used by the new generations of poets in a more literary and generalised language than the dialect which is their mother tongue. There lies my optimism. Faith in the new literary Scots that can be created on the base of the ever-changing regional spoken Scots dialects. This literary Scots will, as always, draw in the literary and dictionary Scots as necessary.

There is, of course, the danger that fewer new words will form than older ones that die and so there will be a move towards standardisation; towards a more anglicised Scots. But we do not know if this is happening in very recent times when there has been a more liberal attitude in educational circles to regional dialects than prevailed even as recently as the fifties. A movement to standardisation may be what practical sensible people would expect to happen given today's social and communication conditions. However it will still be the new Scots with distinctive vocabulary and sounds and syntactic rules. My own literary Scots is generally more anglicised in vocabulary than the spoken Scots of my grandfather, but it is still Scots and I can draw in the old and the new words depending upon my literary needs or on my intention or what comes into my head as I write. Some parts of my work in fact have drawn on older forms more than the critics recognise. Critics generally are bad at vocabulary content of a literary language if that language is created with real skill to sound or read natural. A lot of critics were deceived into thinking Robert Garioch's poetry was written in spoken Edinburgh or Lothian Scots. It was in fact a created literary language which drew in literary and dictionary Scots. I do the same even if my Scots is overall less dense in Scots vocabulary than Garioch's. But I can vary my literary language. My poem 'Weddercock' is an exceptionally obvious example of my using a more extended Scots vocabulary. But it is a rural poem and, also, I set the poem in 1910 although the form of the poem is of my time. But the use of older words can be seen throughout my work despite my general tendency to use a less strong distinctively Scots vocabulary. I believe that, on the strong base of a language founded on contemporary spoken Scots, literary or dictionary Scots can be judicially introduced to a poem without putting a strain on the poetry. Assuming that a poet has the technique to do it. As I say, I've done it more often than critics acknowledge, even if the literary or dictionary words are usually quite well distributed throughout a long poem or a group of short ones.

I believe optimism to be an essential for the future of literary Scots. The spoken dialects will go their own stubborn, independent ways. But without that optimism that leads to educating and writing and publishing, we let the language languish and decline and eventually die as an adult, intelligent and imaginative literary medium. If MacDiarmid had been pessimistic about Scots in the twenties we would not have had the great Scots poetry of this century. If I had been pessimistic about Scots when I founded *Akros* and Akros Publications in the sixties we might not have had a third wave of Scots-writing poets. I could not have written 'A Scots Requiem' such as Christopher Rush's in *Akros* 48 as I do not see languages dying all that easily, although, as I said, I see them changing. I remain true, basically, to a modern anglicised Scots because it is my language, rather than some false-to-me Scots of the past or of areas foreign to me. In my head Scots and Scottish English with a Scottish pronunciation and twist are inseparably intertwined, and in being true to myself I am true to that leid, even if I draw in some literary Scots as well as the Scots I spoke as a boy, so creating my own distinctive literary language. As Donald Campbell said in his poem 'Bilingual Manifesto' (which he kindly inscribed to me) he, like me, is looking for 'an unkent airt whaur baith leids mell and meet'. There is no pessimism in Donald's poem and none in my poetry. We believe in a Scots leid of the present and the future, not of the past. Of course I understand the sadness of older people who see the Scots they know decline. I am a little sad that today's school children don't speak of 'plunkin' the school. They do, however, it seems 'plug' it. It is also sad to me that they probably don't see speugies on the wires but wee sparrows. But they have their own distinctive Scots words. But on the literary front, quoting from an essay by Walter Bernhart in *Akros* 38, August 1978, we Scottish writers who have accepted or forged a form of bilingualism – mixed Scots – have established links with European poets 'unique', says Bernhart, since the days of the auld makars. He also writes: 'This "New Harmony" of the two languages, which was envisaged by Duncan Glen in 1975 (*Akros* 27) and found its poetic definition in Donald Campbell's "Bilingual Manifesto" (*Akros* 33, 1977), appears to be the most significant development in Scottish poetry since Hugh MacDiarmid's early activity'. One of the poems Dr Bernhart singled out as a good example of the 'integration of the languages' was one by me printed in *Akros* 37 under a pseudonym and under the title 'Homer Country' although it is part of my *On Midsummer Evenin Merriest of Nichts?* The poem reads:

This is Homer country.
Here by the seaside in cemetery in Fife.

Then death will drift upon me
from seaward, mild as air, mild as your hand. [1]

The meenister's words into the wund
aulder than time they seem.
And pop sang birlin in my heid
Through the graves the wind is blowing.
And him of perfect physique
and not quite twenty
being lowered to be at ane wi the mool
as his stane in time
carved in immemorial leid

from seaward, mild as air, mild as your hand . . .

The one-time Scottish Renaissance creed that major poetry can only
be written in a Scots of an extended vocabulary is obviously nonsense
and I have already stated my views on that in relation to my own
poetry. What was wrong with post-Burnsian and pre-MacDiarmidian
poetry was not essentially the vocabulary, although that was also
stereotyped, but the sentimentality and parochialness, the lack of
poetic ambition, technique and imagination – the lack of important
poets writing in Scots and within the tradition with high aims and
wishing to 'make it new'. Like MacDiarmid we need some arrogance,
some faith in ourselves and our Scottish traditions. We may fail but at
least we can commit ourselves to all-out, uncompromised effort – we
can aim high. I am all for the doers. To quote Pound, 'this is not
vanity/Here error is all in the not done,/all in the diffidence that
faltered . . .' So I believe optimistically that if great poetry can be
written by Englishmen or Irishmen or Americans in their forms of
English, so then Scotsmen can write great poetry in an anglicised Scots
if that is their true-to-themselves language. Since the eighteenth century, as MacDiarmid said, 'Scots includes English'. Mind you I say an
anglicised Scots, which my own poetry is seen today as being written
in, but it has to be remembered that the sounds are Scots throughout
my poetry unless, for example, I assume the voice of polite anglicised
or English-educated Scots for reasons of, say, humour or pomposity or
polite (so-called) formality or foreignness. Someone said in a review
that I was more interested in ideas than in words. This is not true. I am
fascinated by ideas but I am equally fascinated by the sound patterns
that emerge as I write my poetry. As with vocabulary, many critics are
not good at noting subtle sound patterns in a language which, due to
the skill of the poet, reads easily and naturally. Anyway the sound
patterns of my poetry are dependent on even my English-looking

[1] *Odyssey*, Book XXIII.

words being given the proper Scots pronunciation. This is vital to me and to my poetry. Turn my poetry into English sounds and the sound patterns, the music, goes. My own belief is that quite a few Lowland Scottish writers change the sounds of their language between 'hearing it in their heads and putting it down in English forms on the paper. I was very interested to see a newcomer to poetry, Stewart McGavin, point out in *Akros* 48 that he had noticed that some Scottish writers of 'English' 'translate into something close to Scots as they read. It is not just accent as such things as verb endings are changed.' It seems to me that such writers of what many readers take as English English are risking the music of their poetry by not recognising and indicating in some way that the sounds they are writing are not English sounds. Of course I risk mutilation of my sound patterns by not adopting a phonetic or more Scottish spelling in my poems. Northern English writers like Basil Bunting have the same problem and, indeed, even Wordsworth could be said to have had this problem. But the language question has been so controversial and political and social in Scotland that the debate goes round and round in circles. First of all MacDiarmid is attacked for writing poems in an extended Scots vocabulary. Now, because he succeeded in that, although he wrote great poems in all kinds of Scots and mixtures of Scots and English and in Scottish English, we get people like me attacked for not using an obviously extended Scots vocabulary. Great poetry can be written using an elaborate vocabulary or in a language with an austere vocabulary. Poets go their own ways and if they succeed they can prove or disprove any theory. The menaces are the authoritarians who would try to impose their method as the only right one. I do not disapprove of those who use a more extended Scots vocabulary than I do so long as they write achieved poetry and not just dead language on the page. Alastair Mackie uses such an extended language and, indeed, was attacked recently for self-indulgence over the sounds of Scots words. But coming from Aberdeen of the twenties and thirties Alastair has a stronger Scots vocabulary to his speech base than most Scots today. So he is being true to himself although he does, of course, draw in literary and dictionary Scots. Thus he fights for the Scots language by creating true poetry in it as, indeed, does Christopher Rush despite his 'A Scots Requiem' which I printed in *Akros* for its poetry, notwithstanding its pessimistic stance.

But we need more editors and teachers, politicians and publishers, as well as writers who are optimistic and confident about Scots. Some people, including some publishers influenced by London publishing attitudes, find it hard to believe how much demand there is for poetry in Scots. As I have already said, the sales of books published by Akros

Publications proves that there is this demand. Alex Scott's *Cantrips*, Alastair Mackie's *Clytach* and my own *In Appearances* all sold out quickly. Scots, it has to be remembered, is still *the* emotive language of the Lowland Scot.

Not, of course, having said that, that I am suggesting that we return to an easy, sentimental, sound-only Scots. The intellection which MacDiarmid put back into the Scots tradition has to be maintained. I am tempted to end this chapter by quoting my poem in defence of Scots, 'A Selection of Language', which is in my *Gaitherings* but instead I shall quote an extract from *The State of Scotland* where I address the American poet Louis Zukofsky and where I do not underestimate, I think, the importance of sound in poetry but stress some of the other important factors.

> Titles I am not good
> at mindin.
> But your
> *A!*
> That is
> eh . . .
> And what
> of aaaah?
> Joy in recognition?
> The witch in the sound
> (which?)
> dancin round the bubblin, bilin pot.
> But joy
> in sensory sound sighin and ploppin
> out
> the sense, sicht
> aaahnd
> – intellection.

CHAPTER 23

Poet at Work

In *Appearances* seems to be the starting point of my work for critics although personally I am pleased with a few poems that appear in *Kythings* but are not reprinted in *In Appearances* and as I write this one or two correspondents seem to have rediscovered my *Idols*. When I wrote *In Appearances* I did not have a doubt in my head that I would be given the words to finish it. I truly slaved at it and at one time it must have been four times its final length. Alexander Scott has written of the poem being composed over a long time span, but in fact most of the time I spent on it was cutting, extending and cutting again, arranging and re-arranging material already written. The actual words and form of the poems that survive were written over a quite short space of time except for section 5 which was written after the rest of what is in the final form. My *Realities Poems* was written over a much longer period so far as the actual writing was concerned and kept on growing and growing, although during the months or years of its writing again I was in a confident state of mind so far as the poetry went and, indeed, with regard to life in general. A poet's states of mind count for nothing in the final judgment of what is eventually published but something of my exuberant confidence can perhaps be detected in the section of *In Appearances* simply entitled 'Poet' which I quote in full:

POET

Here again in this cauld place
a fraim alane and silent, I
look for her I strauchle for
through the daurk shadows and drumlie clouds
found in thochts and wan pages
steppin heavy through
aa thae burns
and bins and bins. Turnin sounds
that keep out her voice
and blin to the words
seen clear when written.

I am auld and alane. I fecht
frae turnin to auld freends
left ahint and shoutin

for a return to hame;
to the country we ken;
the schule and kirk; muckle
choirs wi lean soloists
praisin ae God and
our fellows wha hae nae dout
we are aa His sons.

But she's Alba's Eurydice
in unkent country. A place
o heicher bins and caulder lifts
abune this happt path
and drowie clouds.
She caas across thae auld pages
o warm stanes on bare bins
and a blue sky that is open
abune the wund and rain.

I hear o her in Dante, and Henryson
e'en. In Milton, and Virgil.
And Orpheus warns
that the dwaum gaes again
wi backward looks. She belangs
no then, but nou, a Eurydice
waitin an Orpheus
wha sees the endless path
and hears the completin voice . . .

But
I hae nocht to dae
wi Styx;
I can bide on Clyde and that's the wey
to ony Hell.
I hae nae Latin, nor Greek, nor drunk frae
Hippocrene Spring.
And thae bins? Thae hae nocht to dae
wi Helicon Hill!

Aye! . . . Aye!
I hae nocht to say o Apollo's kin
nor Pluto's weys
wi ravished Proserpina nou I min
aa thae Gods stappt doun our throats
as Education
– that Scottish God that stots and creeps
through Gallic Wars,
Ulysses, and aa thae het-up myths o you yersel
wha's name I canna tell
– though ken
as mysel.

You can lie unner Eildon Tree nae dout
wi Thomas –
or Smith for the maitter o it –
but I would walk you out;
meikle bins and twistit roads dancin
foolish agin the lift
– and lang unkent steps rinnin
to tunes I canna mind for singin.

I hae grey hair that rises to your cry,
as weill you ken,
and a hallickit hert;
an auld wud ane thuddin, though aye
waitin slaw and sleekit to run
owre that road wi you
whaur clods race for the fun
o that huntin wun.

I maun gang walkin out to glower
at the mune
and licht on the midden. And lauch
wi you that points out the glaur
– and smell – and that deid cat
hingin frae the waa; its tail a cleik
and een aince fat
for clegs and craws and ither cat.

Here's faur frae Huntly Bank. Here's glaur –
and waur aye! –
but there's flouers I ken as green and reid
though my een are baith waur
and better wi aa your licht
– and thae braw weeds at my heid.
And you lauchin out sae bricht
– at me lyin in the munelicht.

But I bring you bins live wi fechtin fun
and scuddin
– aye scuddin! – clouds that come and gae
as dinner frae your haunds
– and see the braw autumn reids
and saft yellows in muck frae byre
and rats heids
lichtit on the midden wi aa thae seeds.

And the joy I experienced in writing the whole of *Realities Poems* is
perhaps seen in the final section of 'The Inextinguishable' which is Part
13 of the book.

I sing of the young mavis in the green green
meadows and the laverock free free.
Sing sing o the pure caller air
and rime on the pastures
and skaters on the pond.
And Sundays in toun wi the ringin o bells
but backgrun to freedom
to sit in the park and think as you will.
I walk to the taps and new symphonies
kent as if classics o the past
vibratin in the cauld clear air
to reach to the heichs imaginable
and taen as if gien for us alane
and yet haudin in its risin sound
aa that is man true to himsel.

Sing sing o the young mavis
and the laverock risin free, free
sing o the steep steep side to be faced and,
creation itsel,
aye a challenge to order
as it has been and is.

Tarra ra

The bairn in the cot and new thocht
to become man aa thocht
and sang and dance and
luve.
I sing o luve makin aa
new.
And the fresh caller air
owre aathing
wi the skaters on the pond
and man atap the unscalable peak.

Tarra ra

I sing of you my luve
and aa we hae thocht
and done
in luve. The clear
thocht
seen thegither or apairt
but jined as ane
for aa the individual
separateness.
I sing. I sing
of man and woman

thegither
and a glisk o that movin licht
that jines
aa to aa.

I see you
Man
jined to aa that is.
Sing sing sing
o the clear throatit sang
that is truth and beauty
and thocht itsel
risin
to staun brichter than ony staur
or sun.

Tarra ra
Tarra ra ra
Tarra ra ra
Tarra ra

I sing o the perfect circle.
That girl
bent owre her bairn
and owre the hay
and the hairvest in
and the field ploughed
straucht
for next season.
And I walk the auld toun
in the Spring
wi warmth on my back
and sit in the sun
and see aa that is
passin as the seasons
and the sun there
risin and settin
and you and me
thegither
thegither.
I sing o man
himsel
heich
on the heichest ben
o thocht
and luve.
Sing

o the mavis
in the meadow
and laverock
risin
singin
free

free
free

free

Duncan Glen with his children Ian and Alison in garden at Penwortham July 1968.

CHAPTER 24

Penwortham

WHEN I left Glasgow and my authoritarian boss in 1965 it was to return to education, unfortunately not in Scotland with the opportunity of helping to establish an educational base for Scottish culture. I went as a lecturer in graphic design to the Harris College which became, as already said, Preston Polytechnic. I stayed there from 1965 to 1978 and helped to establish from virtually nothing what is now a very-well-thought-of BA(Hons) course in graphic design. It is a sandwich course, with students in real employment for six months of the course, and was the first such in graphic design in the country. I really slaved finding sandwich placements for the students with publishers and printers but I did achieve promotions for my trouble, progressing from Lecturer II to Senior Lecturer to Principal Lecturer to Head of Graphic Design. Whilst at Preston I established the Harris Press for the college and printed quite a range of pamphlets, from Hugh MacDiarmid's *On a Raised Beach* (with four-colour illustrations by Alan Powell) to a history of a church building, my own humorous *Five Literati* and an analysis of Ted Hughes' *Gaudete*. When *On a Raised Beach* was published MacDiarmid wrote to me on 20th July 1967: 'The production exceeds even my expectations'. Whilst at Preston I also edited the annual magazine *Graphic Lines*.

We did not have a large garden in Penwortham – some two miles from Preston – but it was bounded on one side by a tree-lined burn and it became quite powerful in my imagination. The sequence 'Traivellin Man' in *Realities Poems* starts and finishes in that garden. The first poem reads:

I

WAIT FOR THE HOUR

To curb the fretful bairn and trust the blood
WILLIAM SOUTAR

Aince I hae been a traivellin man.

Have bag will travel. Aye mair like a tourist
than a native resident. Movin on every twa years
at least and makin several important journeys each year
to different places.

Nou I sit in this gairden day efter day
The Guardian shadin my een frae the sun
wi our boundary burn murmellin on my nerves
and the mavis disturbin the haill
neibourhood.

I tak an occasional daunder round the lawn,
near every five minutes in fact,
and throw lumps o sile at our cat
stalkin birds in the flouer beds. I hae

mony restless thochts and memories in my heid
but the future's an enless line o deckchairs,
shut in this gairden day efter day. It's nae life
for a traivellin man wi ideas in his heid

waitin to tak flicht.

In fact at that time I had an abundance of poetic ideas which took
flight.

My long poem *On Midsummer Evenin Merriest of Nichts?* published
in 1981 could be said to have its base in a garden – perhaps my
Penwortham garden if you want a realist geography for the poem
although of course the garden is also that of the imagination. The poem
begins:

You caa, my luve, I ken not what
as I sit this Midsummer
evenin . . .

I face a sma rectangle of whiteness
A4,
in this gairden of delicht
and of dule
as time taks its turn . . .

and this form gien to me . . .

Poets always hope that the latest form given to them will be true to
the perfect form they have in their heads, as Blake said, but at the same
time they are divided towards wishing their latest work to be recognised and their earlier work not to be underestimated. So I am torn
when in a review of *On Midsummer Evenin Merriest of Nichts?*, in
Lines Review 80 (March 1982) Donald Campbell saw the poem as
being my 'most successful creation to date. This is so, I believe, very
largely because of the economy of the poem's structure, which concen-
trates the utterance within a single imagined moment. We are asked to
accept that the poem takes place between the sound of the poet's wife

calling him and his reply – although we never actually find out what they are saying to each other.' I also see it as, to use a dangerous word in that it can be misunderstood, the Muse as well as my wife who is calling and the poem is the result of what she inspires me to give form to. But I hope someone will sort all that out for me as it is not the job of the poet to explain his poems.

But in even more recent poems our Penwortham garden pops up. As for example in a poem written on 12th September 1982 as part of my sequence *The Turn of the Earth:*

OUR GAIRDEN

You and I movin thegither
in our gairden of delight.

Our gairden lined to the faur horizon
wi aik, sycamore and ash.

And the great tree at its centre
jinin to heiven and earth.

And murmellin burn aye flows through it
and aa the birds o the air sing for us.

You caa me times without end
to our gairden.

A gairden ayont description
or leid e'en out of the air.

And yet but a sma patch
you tend and keep each week for it and us

as you and I
at our ease close thegither.

Perhaps the great tree besides being a large apple tree in my real garden is also the Great Tree Yggdrasill, but again it is for others to make what they can of the poem and the whole sequence.

Lancashire, like my native industrial Lanarkshire, is often thought of, by those who do not know it, as an industrial waste-land and without doubt it is in parts, but we walked very many beautiful rural parts of Lancashire and *On Midsummer Evenin Merriest of Nichts?* has a small section arising out of an absolute-seeming silence I 'heard' on one of these walks:

Nou walkin the country lanes
o Lancashire
or whaurever you tak it nou –

this gemm of the life of poetry . . .

Surprised by stillness – and the sound of silence
there's naethin but this Summer day's time.
Aa is new and fresh as mavis's kent sang
in the throat of this surroundin silence.

Walk the side-roads edged by green paths
and touch the white dog-rose blossom. Gone
are the memories of past sadness
or fear of themorrow's endins to come.

Only the present is touched in the stillness
and ilka step a Summer day's dance.
Each braith a new-felt rhythm
and aa is close to what is true to aa.

And pause by sma stane brig. Look doun
to fast-rinnin burn turnin white owre stanes
soon gone wi the stillness and the silence.
And nou a sad sang owre that single day?

My daughter Alison was born in Preston and I wrote a poem of her
baby days:

WI A FAITHER'S EEN
(To Alison)

You sit. A tea-cosy bricht in braw blue.
A scallopt jaicket. A Chelsea china piece
Or daintee German doll and Goya figure too.

And nou. A pentit clockwork toy rockin back
And furrit wi wild talk wound out
As sound frae Injuns on a film track.

Or ane o thae wechtit toys that faas and faas,
But canna stey put though knockt aa about
The heid bairnlike, wi thochtless dunts and blaws.

Poet talk! A fancy tea-cosy toy wi nocht seen
O ony nappie. A doll that turns and kicks
Aa blin afore thae daurk and open een.

Alison also features in *On Midsummer Evenin Merriest of Nichts?* as
a small girl very interested in birds:

He's but twa fit frae our windae
As mony anither day.
'A wren in the snow-in-summer'

To you I murmur,
But he's gone. You are but five
And very, very much alive.
But I feel the cauld
And see you white-haired and auld.
I'm gone as wren
I ken.

That is a rather sad little section of *On Midsummer Evenin Merriest of Nichts?* and although I see it as essentially a work of joy, only with some inevitable sadness, I have been accused of being very concerned in this work with regret for days that are gone and the irrecoverability of the past. Certainly this is to be seen in a section which involves both my children:

I think of times quickly gone in prams and cots
and of first steps and first words.
Of new bicycle and party dresses.
And wild parties wi jelly and cream.

'Forget the past' I hear you say
'and lingering thochts'. Memories
of first days and me in white coat and mask
aside your mither's hospital bed.

I think of a short Spring soon gone
and of my high Summer – busy makin a career!

I do not see myself as a sad or depressive person, although I did have one spell of quite acute depression whilst living in Penwortham, due largely to overwork and too much responsibility at the Polytechnic. I wrote a sequence of poems at this time – or just after it – entitled 'Sad Sequence', the second part of which reads:

II

THE TIMES LIE HEAVY

The times lie heavy
aa is a container o sorrow
mornin brings the thocht o lang day
the evenin the anticipation o sleepless 'ours
and the brou is weet wi sweit.

I hear sadness in bricht tunes
I see daith in the livin mither
I feel the jag o pain in relief frae it;
the house full o daurk memories
and walks alive wi past sorrows.

Folk pass in grey monotony
and loved anes a drag to talk to.
Aa joy is lost in the sadness
o the endless 'ours stretchin
on and on to a sad eternity.

But since I came through that experience I have considered myself
very fortunate, contented and unstressful. Indeed in a poem I have
seen myself, even if a little humorously, as being in a state of non-
religious 'grace'. The poem is from 'Ane to Anither' from *Realities
Poems:*

IV

GRACE

Here in the warm sun o your luve
it seems owre easy to claim open communication.

But I hae a wey wi e'en casual acquaintances.
I seem to see richt through folk.
I look into a pair o een
and it's as if I ken him better than himsel
or what he'd admit to himsel!
I see hatred o me in flashin een
and spitefu voice
but feel nae anger or e'en real regret
takin it for a sorrow.
I see whit's really ahint thae words meant to hurt.
It's as if I had a skin like a hippo.
I accept aa as they come
though try to let them see the joy
o union ane wi anither. But
I hae nae real missionary speerit
kennin they may be like me ane day
– at their ease
in a state o kennin acceptance.

I feel as if aa naitur is my kin
and hae to mind mysel o the savagery
in the wild. A flouer I dinna speak to
but cut wi muckle reluctance and chase
the germ-cairryin blue-bottle out the windae.
It seems aa hae a richt to their particular weys
and I feel union wi them aa . . .
man, wumman, child,
black, white, yellow
aa belang to being,
life to life.

This pouer struck me sudden. Sometimes I think
I maun be in a state o
grace. It's no as if I warked for it or at it,
this peace and unnerstaundin.
I canna claim to be deservin o it
but I hae it
it seems.

I'm quite a holy man
on the quait
– it drives folk mad.

To revert to my sense of nostalgia for the past, perhaps, like not a
few poets, I am wary of my past being truly lost – to me that is – and
try to let it live through language. Certainly memory is important to me
as the quotation from Carlos Williams at the front of this book perhaps
reveals – as indeed does another poem I wrote in September 1982 –
again part of *The Turn of the Earth*. But the poem is also perhaps
about, amongst yet other things, the fear during a fallow period of
poems not ever again being 'given' as we 'sit, only sittin':

THE MAKAR

I sit, only sittin.

I sit astride warrior's great horse
and twa ravens flee owre my heid.

But I faa to the ground
and knot is tied in my heid.

I am bound round and round
as I face the approachin wolves

and the black birds
ready to swoop.

I sit, only sittin.

I sit atap the meikle bin
and twa ravens flee round my heid.

Thocht and Memory
fleein aff owre the haill warld.

Yet fear for them.
Will they return?

As I sit, only sittin.

CHAPTER 25

The Inheritors

WHILST I do not believe, as I have said, that society should demand that poets speak for it, it is often true, of course, that even when going their own way poets reflect their time. Our time is unique in that the whole planet could be destroyed tomorrow. So I have written an anti-bomb poem, 'Out of a Clear Blue Sky'. I have, of course, written social poems which reflect the way of life of the Cambuslang of my childhood. I have also written *Clydesdale* which is perhaps a historical social poem and there are other social poems such as 'Sunday Mornin in Shared Village Gairden' which Barry Wood picked out for its 'nice ironies and formal grace'. In my mind I link this poem with another. 'The Inheritors' which Alexander Scott described as 'an especially striking tour de force'.

SUNDAY MORNIN IN A SHARED VILLAGE GAIRDEN

It should be
a peacefu scene. Neibours in a shared gairden
and the sun on our backs. Cool green shade
and a blue heatit pool.
Ours is an aa-electric village.

It's true
there's a fecht gaein on. The auld blackie
his grey feathers hingin doun
has a warld at stake
agin a shiny young aggressor.

It's true
the young couple hae their radio owre loud
I'd guess they're hie wi pot
and it's obvious
she's taen the tap aff her wee bikini.

It's true
the learnit maister o science is a man
o the academy. He seriously thinks
he's communicatin to them
his angst
for aa his silence and shut een.

    It's true
he's communicatin wi me. They're serious
in themsels   locally shut aff
for aa the warld's communications in their lugs
    and the noisy
communication o their style.

    It's true
I'm a spectator still pleyin gemms to pass
awa my time   though we've gien them up
wi wark as guid in themsels.
    We are the elect;
simplicity come out o selective complexity.

    Nou
they've switched aff their radio
and pose to meditate in the auld yogi style.
Are they showin their shiny fethers efter aa?
    Or conflict
lowered e'en lower wi'in themsels?

Or the second law o thermodynamics?

    The slaw
run doun at wark in us for aa the dense layers
o thocht we've built up and satellites
    broadcastin
our reflections round the curve o the earth.

    Or energy
increased in peace. Aa in aa
out o the gropin in the daurkness directin
to the aa in ane. It's true a simple
    sunny
Sunday mornin in a shared village gairden.

    And yet
this is a new village aside the auld. The blackie's
territorial war is naethin new   if owre
for the minute and seen to hae
    a wrocht pettern
for aa the passin complexities o the fecht

that's nou seen
    simply
as bein
    a dance towards luve.

THE INHERITORS
For aa the dangers o crossin the road
    the fearful percentages for cancer
the bomb cloudin our lifts
    the threatenin wudness for ane in ten
for aa the lives cut aff   we are the lucky anes

            the survivors
the inheritors   the elect   we are
    and uniquely oursels
we hae made it into the sun   we escaped
    the naitural abortions   (and the unnaitural
    wi civilisation as it is)
the miscairriages that deprive sae many millions
    o what we caa our life

the codit information wi the potential
    for a thousand Dantes   gane

the true misfits o our kind   rejectit yet
    unique to themsels
in the womb   the pettern o the chromosomes
    naitural selection protectin Homo Primatura
frae its genetic errors   a triumph for heredity
    orderin the chemicals that jine us to
livin naitur   the dust on earth, the cosmos
    and rejects the misfits.

The millions o millions rejectit yet individual
    ayont the common pettern
e'en if but for a day   efter the creation.
    Unique
to the shape o our face   the colour o our een
    decidit when seed met egg.

        Nae quick daith can tak that frae them
        e'en if anelie kent efter daith
    or flushed awa unrecognised   in sad horror.

            But
gien mair time there's the individual experiences o life
    in the womb.
The original egg   complex as life itsel and fou
    wi the greatest potential
if for an unfulfillt future
    e'en a Dante regrets the boy's potential
for aa his later rich maturity.

We are the lucky anes   the inheritors
    the experiences o life efter birth
shapin us further in our uniqueness
    if that rich code unfulfillt agin its potential
and aa the pain and deformities cairrit
    to daith.

                        Yet
        we are the lucky anes
    we can dance a dance o gledness
        we are the unique anes

    what's the shape o a face or colour in the ee
        without anither to catch the returnin glance
    uniquely hersel
        as aa the warld spins round our heids.

Duncan looking out to his garden from his study window. Used on cover of his book On Midsummer Evenin Merriest of Nichts? *Photograph by* Euan Duff.

CHAPTER 26

Nottingham

I LEFT Preston Polytechnic in late April 1978 with good feelings both for the institution, where I had helped to push forward an educational idea of a degree-level sandwich course in graphic design, and for the town of Preston and the suburb of Penwortham where I had led such an active life as husband, father, poet, critic, editor, publisher and lecturer in graphic design. For the last issue of *Akros* from Penwortham I printed a group of Preston poems, including my own 'Penwortham' which is the final poem of the sequence 'Traivellin Man'. As I have already made obvious, this sequence, like fourteen others, is part of *Realities Poems*. This book was published in Nottingham but all of it was written at 14 Parklands Avenue, Penwortham, as, indeed, was all my published poetry up to *Realities Poems* and in fact including some of *On Midsummer Evenin Merriest of Nichts?* although that work was given its final form in Radcliffe-on-Trent, Nottingham.

As I have said, what a joy was that period of writing the poetry that comprises *Realities Poems*. And most people who have written on it have been very kind. George Bruce, for example, wrote in *Lines Review*: 'A poem of consequence to the Scottish Renaissance, a poem of large and sustained purpose . . . Glen has extended the literary sensibility in Scots. This is the occasion for the celebration of an achievement of distinction.' But in a sense I remember the writing and the publication of my first truly organised (to my mind) book of poetry, *In Appearances*, 1971, as even more of a celebration for me personally. This is, I suppose, because it was the first collection which I was happy with, although I was very grateful to Caithness Books for previously publishing *Kythings* in which many extracts from *In Appearances* were printed. One of the first pleasures I had when *In Appearances* was published was a letter out of the blue from someone whose name I cannot now remember, asking my permission to publish some translations of my poems into Spanish. This letter was not from Spain but from somewhere in Central America, Panama I think, and I have wondered how he got hold of a copy of the book so quickly. But I was also fortunate enough to get very kind reviews, including one by Anne Cluysenaar in *Stand*. I had admired her critical writings so it was very pleasant to read her words: 'Duncan Glen, also a Scottish poet and editor of *Akros*, is already, in his late thirties, a very considerable poet.

In Appearances is an eighty-page work made up of connected and developing poem-clusters and concluded by a ten-page imaginary autobiography. The whole defines a highly articulated life-view.'

Most critics have seen *In Appearances* as a unified whole but inevitably some of the poems which form the clusters have become known as separate poems. The most famous, and most anthologised and most broadcast is 'My Faither'. I wrote the poem to its finished state during a train journey from Edinburgh to Preston. I do not know how or when in the writing I 'thought' of the change of spelling of 'My faither' to 'My father' in the last stanza. Christopher Rush in an essay 'Younger Writers in Scots' in *Akros* 45 (December 1980) wrote: 'The short refrain at the end of each quatrain tightens the screw of an accumulative emotional tension that is reminiscent of certain ballad refrains. The switch to English in the final line (compare the last line of "Lord Randal" where a sudden switch from the established verbal pattern detonates the poem) is a touch of genius.'

There is a two-page criticism of the poem by Michael K. Glenday in *Akros* 51 (October 1973) which ends most kindly by referring the reader to:

'The cumulative power of the poem's language itself, a Scots idiom which is lapidary and solid-sounding and which, robust as the "black shinin range", is a medium commensurate with the immutability of the son's vision. In a sense the items of clothing, totemic as they are, do not matter (so much is ironically apparent in the "weel chosen" funereal garb of the last stanza); what does matter is that the poem communicates through a deceptively effortless and assured diction and that this authority becomes associated not only with the form but also with the subject, "my faither". Glen uses the last word of the poem to draw attention to his use of language and there, if not before, we understand how fully the poem's subject has been created out of style and rhetoric.

The last stanza shows the dramatic integration of language, technique, and meaning. Without his "lum hat" and no longer attired in the informality of "galluses and nae collar/For the flannel shirt" we see that the cloth of death covers a most terrible absence. Disaffiliation, estrangement, and a dramatic sense of loss are all conveyed in the anglicization of the last word, a word empty of much more than its one, dropped letter. And yet, though I began by comparing Glen and MacDiarmid as elegists, "My Faither" does not register the language of grief. Its voice, though elegiac, is not freighted with sorrow as is that of, say, Carlos Williams in 'The Widow's Lament in Springtime". Nor, thankfully, does it ring with the mock-gaiety of a wake. It was F. Scott Fitzgerald who once averred that "the love of life is essentially as incommunicable as grief.'' Somehow, the voice of "My Faither" contrives to combine the two emotions, expressing their mutality.'

The poem reads:

MY FAITHER

Staunin nou aside his braw bress-haunled coffin
I mind him fine aside the black shinin range
In his grey strippit trousers, galluses and nae collar
For the flannel shirt. My faither.

I ken him fine thae twenty or mair years ago
Wi his great bauchles and flet auld kep;
And in his pouch the spottit reid neepkin
For usin wi snuff. My faither.

And ben in the lobby abune the braw shoon and spats
Aside the silk waistcoat and claw-haimmer jaicket
Wi its muckle oxter pouch, hung the lum hat.
They caa'd him Jock the Lum. My faither.

And nou staunin wi the braw shinin haunles
See him and me baith laid out in the best
Black suitin wi proper white aa weel chosen.
And dinna ken him. *My father.*

No matter how happy we may be in our personal relationships we all have strong feelings of loneliness at some time. I have already quoted my poem 'Poet' which begins, 'Here again in this cauld place/a fraim alane and silent' and there is a section on the river of poetry in *Mr & Mrs J. L. Stoddart at Home* which begins with the lines, 'The makar stauns alane/without feres'. I would quote this section as an expression, when I wrote these words, of how I saw the poet in the river of creativity.

The makar stauns alane
without feres
and desires the river flowin past
as me you.
A faur-gone Clyde I ken wi mysel
wi watters come frae sources
or burns or God kens whaur –

and that jaup thrown by risin trout
or drappin stane. Whaur does it gae
nou it's come and's gaein?
Whaur does it come out?

We maun staun heich in the river and tak the watters
flowin by as nou.
      Our present taen wi joy.

We hae a new pettern formin unkent
and yet the body steerin the ripples
mair nor it thinks
for aa the strength o the flowin currents.

Dams are there to be made wi body and mind
and watterfaas creatit for our pleisure. The stane thrown, and
trout loured
wi a weill-dresst flee
if sometimes lowpin for the fun of it
            it seems
                – to our joy!

The river flows on
for aa it is ours in the watter round us
– and has to be focht for.

Doun to the sea it drives
for aa our savin diversions
and is here to staun against
and feel the clean new currents
on our bodies.

But the new-formed petterns hae to be seen
apairt frae the rinnin tide. Mindit,
and guidit, upstream and doun
till raised new abune the rabblement o the watters
that whisper mony sangs at aince
o past and present. On the faur bank mony voices jaubber
and rise ane agin the ither. I staun mysel,
alane, yet at ane wi the present river.
I'm struisslin agin the tellin currents. I brace
agin strang races rinnin for stagnant creeks and pules.
Lie agin broad watters lined wi sma waves
pushin for weirs sterile for aa the reemin watters. And
yet aa taen up in the movin pettern.
A warld raised abune the river
and new and passed on
           – if aye flowin into new watters.

We can jine haunds across the river
and feel the tide rise on us thegither
for aa we are oursels
and unique in the flowin river
each new day.

> I turn again to you, as the river, and we splash
> in the clear blue watter...
>
> and shout wi joy...

So it turns out to be a love poem as well and so a poem not of isolation but of togetherness. But there is also the loneliness and a poet certainly may feel alone as he writes. Indeed, it is also difficult for many poets of today not to feel isolated from their own society. Certainly this is revealed in much modern poetry and certainly sometimes it comes through in mine. In a review in *Stand* of *A Cled Score* (1974), the poems from which are reprinted in my *Gaitherings* (1977) as is *Clydesdale*, 1971, and the poems of *Feres*, 1971, Desmond Graham wrote:

> ' "Graduation", "At a Poetry Readin in the Local Schule", and "Sunday Morning in a Shared Village Gairden" play on the emptiness of modern social life and Glen's separation from it, with equal deftness. And Glen sustains his evocation of industrial Clydeside and his childhood there, in the long meditative poem which closes the volume, "A Journey Past", by a gentle probing of his own place in the scene:

> > I hae great feelin
> > for the place
> > peerin out the windae.
> > You micht say it is *my*
> > place. I hae sent doun
> > rutes
> > for aa the times I've been
> > uprutit
> > yet there's thae wee white anes
> > that feed my mind
> > and mak reality
> > in the imagination.

> Glen's touch is so light that one is hesitant about offering exposition for fear of looking heavy-handed. But it is remarkable how unobtrusively he has restored to direct experience the age-old paradox of reality and imagination. He has taken the range and scale of the "makar" through a triumph of tone, an ability in the first three of these lines to assure the reader that self-irony has been too well learnt to be forgotten... He schools his readers to follow him in leaving judgments open while fully observing their urgency, and his authority grows from a restlessness of mind which turns from statement to statement to take the weight of what is not sayable.'

A poet may feel alone as he writes but one of the advantages he has is that he can feel part of a tradition although he must avoid facile imitation if the tradition is to progress and not get bogged down in repetition as the Scots tradition did between Burns and MacDiarmid. Still all poets are one in a long line that has faced the blank sheet of paper. When I wrote my early poems I had, naturally enough, no sense of being one of a long line but I did get a sense of that when I wrote *Clydesdale* at the end of 1970. That long poem is at one level my history of Cambuslang and I had a very strong sense of history as I wrote it – or after I had written it. I felt, to myself, that in writing it I was a new part of that history.

It pleased me when Ken Edward Smith saw me as one of a line of twentieth-century Scots-writing poets rather than as an isolated poet creating new forms as I have sometimes felt myself to be. In his essay 'Scottish Poetry as I See It 1965-1981' in *Akros* 50 (October 1982) Smith wrote:

> 'Let us start then, with Alexander Scott and Garioch, two second-wave makars who can be seen as links between the MacDiarmid era and much contemporary Scots verse. Both helped to pull the modern Scots tradition away from the synthetic Lallans associated with Sydney Goodsir Smith and Tom Scott. Without denying the merits of these last two it seems fair to claim that the main line of poetic development passes through Scott's and Garioch's attempts to relate aggrandised Scots to Aberdeen and Edinburgh speech respectively.
>
> In many ways their works are very different, yet they have important shared characteristics (to use the present tense about the work of the late Robert Garioch comes naturally). Both for example are highly conscious of the craft of their art; both share a knowledge of pre-MacDiarmid Scots poetry and of Pre-conquest Anglo-Saxon; both are distinguished by their humour and use of Scots deflation; both, one could argue, share with their English contemporaries a scepticism, a suspicion of the grand gesture, constituting a moment of Classicism between the exuberance of MacDiarmid and the experiment of Duncan Glen.'

Ken Smith further discusses the poetry of Alexander Scott and Robert Garioch and then continues:

> 'Robert Garioch's poise and his self-imposed limitations can be seen as characterising an era of consolidation in Scots poetry. That the work of Alastair Mackie is arguably both more uneven and more challenging suggests one reason why we should link him with Duncan Glen as inaugurating a third phase in modern Scots poetry. Yet a distinction should be made. Mackie's work differs

from that of poets younger than himself in having direct access to the vast word-hoard of pre-war Aberdeenshire. He is aware that, even if Scots is very much alive in the playground, it is not the Scots of his youth.

What this produces in his work is a creative tension and dislocation, with a deep sense of loss, change and mortality playing against an extraordinary creative sense of the power in single words and phrases. There is nothing forced about the compressed power of lines such as these from "Pietà":

> Her face was thrawed.
> She wisna aa come.
>
> In the trams o her airms
> the wummin held oot her first bairn.
> It micht hae been a mercat day
> and him for sale.
> Naebody stoppit to niffer.

Controversy surrounds his work, not so much as to its general merit but as to whether the lyrics of *Clytach* or later, longer sequences represent his best work. Here we may simply note that he has demonstrated that universality can be enhanced by economy of means.

With Duncan Glen our sense of work-in-progress intensifies. If the overall bulk of his work can appear uneven we should bear in mind that he is a deliberate risk-taker. In fact, his lesser poems or relative failures are often instructive. But there is significant and extensive achievement, an enlargement of our sense of what is possible in Scots, or in poetry at large, today. Ten years on, the voice of *In Appearances*, questioning and sceptical yet passionate and committed still has the shock of the new; as in the opening "Time's Gane Oot":

> Time's gane oot
> and we hae snibbed the door.
>
> There's dreams I forget
> and reasons I canna traik.
>
> There's thochts and learnin, e'en
> here. Here wi you abune the simmer burn.
>
> I hae memories aa my ain
> mumblins ayont aa sense.

The explorations are pursued more informally in the witty warm *Mr & Mrs J. L. Stoddart at Home* and in the collection *Gaitherings* which includes some of the poet's most communally-centred poetry in *Clydesdale* and *A Journey Past. Realities Poems* breaks yet more new ground with commendable ambition as does the latest work *On Midsummer Evenin Merriest of Nichts?* Personally, I prefer the tauter free verse in evidence up to the mid-seventies but the energy and *panache* of the later work are evidence that Glen is, despite his wide success, still artistically "hungry".'

But, as I have already said, the third wave of modern poetry in Scots does not end with me. It goes on, for example, in the work of Donald Campbell, Walter Perrie, Raymond Vettese, Raymond Falconer, Christopher Rush and W. N. Herbert; and I eagerly await the emergence of other poets.

It was in Penwortham that I first felt in control as a writer although not at ease in that I was ever content with what I had achieved even if sometimes I was pleased for a time. But as Eliot said:

. . .one has only learned to get the better of words
For the thing one no longer has to say, or the way in which
One is no longer disposed to say it.

An unbeatable task master, but as Auden said:

Time that is intolerant
Of the brave and innocent
And indifferent in a week
To a beautiful physique,

Worships language and forgives
Everyone by whom it lives;

So in the final poem of my 'Traivellin Man' – 'Penwortham' – there is both contentment and a recognition that this condition does not last for the writer who remains creative. As MacDiarmid once said to me, if a man is 'at his ease' he has ceased to be a poet. But I am at peace now as I think back to spring in Penwortham as described in my poem:

XIX

PENWORTHAM

*Oh, to be in England
Now that April's there*
ROBERT BROWNING

It is Spring. The daffodils are in bloom.
The gress is growein and I've taen the lawnmower
on its first walk of the year. The bird's on the wing
which is absurd
the wing being on the bird. But the shilfie's

on the bough, the mavis on the gress
and the wren in the snow in simmer
in Penwortham – now!

There's a green sheen spreidin owre aathing
and the forsythia yella aside the flouerin currant
pink agin the clear blue sky.
I feel the sun on my back and touch
the broun, friable sile. I'll sit content
this simmer, *The Guardian* to shade
my een. Aa sweetness, and at my ease
listenin to the burn gently flowin at the fit o this
my tree-lined gairden.
And the occasional word wi my wife
– or corrieneuchin aa the evenin. There's
the welcome visitor frae north and south
in Penwortham – now!

I am weill content
– at least for a day or twa!

But we left Penwortham for me to take up a job in Nottingham at Trent Polytechnic as Head of the Department of Visual Communication. Two degree courses have been approved by the Council for National Academic Awards (CNAA) and established in the department since I took over – BA(Hons) in Information Graphics and BA(Hons) in Photography. The department also offers a BTEC Higher Diploma in Printing. I spoke of my life in Nottingham in 1982 in the interview in *Akros* 50 from which I have already quoted but the pattern of my life was not changed very much by our move to Nottingham; it was not so very different from what it had been in Penwortham.

D.G.   Well I do work hard. As well as being a Head of Department in England's second largest polytechnic I'm at present very involved with the work of the Council for National Academic Awards, visiting colleges and polytechnics, sometimes as chairman of the visiting panel. But I'm quite easily bored and like to be busy, although I do spend quite a lot of time relaxing and listening to music. But I am also a quick worker when I am working. I'm a quick reader – and writer and thinker for that matter. I'm a quick moving and doing person – I make decisions quickly. But I also sleep long hours. I work on editing *Akros* regularly each weekend. I write poetry only when it comes 'given' to me but I write the first drafts, whether it's a single short poem or a long sequence or poem, quickly even if it means working eighteen hours a day for several weeks. I tend to be 'given' poems during holidays when I am relaxing into thinking conducive to poetry. After I've got the first 'finished' draft down I then work on that over quite a long period of time. With long poems I don't usually write many new parts but I delete and make minor alterations. I read and re-read over months until I stop making these small alterations. But the first intensive work is what really counts and that I do with very strong concentration. I also do it quickly, it seems to me, although when I add up the few hours sleep I've had I am often surprised by the many hours I must have put in on the original writing. But the original impulse for poems must be strong and vital. I don't write without that impulse – the feeling that they are there to be written.

I am glad to say that after our move to Nottingham the impulse to poetry still came to me regularly. I was not yet 'at my ease' and indeed may well still be as creatively 'hungry' as Ken Edward Smith suggested I was.[1]

When we first moved to Radcliffe-on-Trent, which is about six miles from Nottingham, in 1978 we bought a large Victorian house which we restored at some expense and great labour by us all, but especially my wife. The house, however, was really too large for us and we moved to a smaller, thirties house after only two years. But that Victorian house has already crept into some of my poems, including reference in *On Midsummer Evenin Merriest of Nichts?* to an old well situated under the floorboards of a breakfast room. And its small garden features in another poem, again part of *The Turn of the Earth*, although the main subject is a gnome which we inherited with the house:

POET'S GAIRDEN GNOME

I am gnome in poet's gairden.

No a new plastic gnome
but dignified reid-broun fireclay ane of great age.

I staun upright wi bent-owre pixie hat.
I hae a lang shovel in my richt haund.

This symbolises that I'll live to bury poet
haein got him to scrieve thae words.

---

[1] Since writing this book I have had an almost continuous outpouring of poetry. Since the publication of *The Stones of Time* in July 1984 I have published: *Nottingham A Poem*, 1984; *Situations*, 1984; *In the Small Hours*, 1984, and *Geeze!*, 1985. *The Turn of the Earth* actually written before *The Stones of Time*, etc is at galley proof stage as I read the first proofs of this autobiography. Very recently I have given what I hope will be the final revision to a huge sequence at present entitled *Tales to be Told*; it is about as long as *Realities Poems* which runs to 191 pages.

Unless someane takes a haimmer to me
and this leid will be the livin time for me
as him.

But the photograph on the cover of *On Midsummer Evenin Merriest of Nichts?* is of the garden of our second house in Radcliffe-on-Trent and that garden has also already featured in poems. In, for example, a section of *The State of Scotland* addressed to the American poet Gary Snyder. It reads:

I face the gairden
yet again.

Ane gloamin time.
An aipple tree is enough.
A pettern of licht and shade
against the daurkenin lift.
But a white slattit seat tae
wi daurk warked ends
cuttin across the tree's lower trunk.
And
the full moon there
huge. It is owre much.
Movin the mind, indeed,
ayont aa the human junk that ties it doun.
Aa the words and books
gone as that tree
at brak of day.
And drappt without e'en
a thocht of them gone
till relivin at ane remove
I mind your words, Gary Snyder,
in the endless mountains
nou
this mid-August at 25 Albert Road window.

CHAPTER 27

In Place of Wark

EARLIER in this book I described how I discovered as a boy the Rembrandt 'A Man in Armour' in the Glasgow Art Galleries and the French paintings also in Glasgow. As a boy I bought a postcard reproduction of 'A Man in Armour' and it is now on the wall of the room in which I am writing and outside on the staircase is a larger reproduction of the painting. Since I first saw that Rembrandt, paintings have been important to me as is perhaps to be expected of a professional graphic designer. Our house is full of paintings and drawings I have been given or commissioned or bought from living artists whom I have known as colleagues or students.

When I am writing my poems I 'see' images in my mind's eye. Often these images are of incidents or scenes from my life although they can be more abstract; sometimes I change them for creative reasons. How poems come to one is not explainable and the strangest things can trigger them off. *Realities Poems* has a section 'In Place of Wark' which is about a drop-out Ph.D. who is an attendant in a major art gallery. This sequence was triggered off by an incident that I saw in the Tate Gallery, London. I was walking round one of the rooms when I saw an attendant put his ball-point pen on top of an elaborate frame round a painting by Matisse. I nearly jumped up and down with excitement and did, in fact, rush around somewhat. I 'knew' a poem there and then although I had not one word of it in my head. But I made notes of the painting and who bequeathed it and other information and got slides of it and other paintings. And when I got home I wrote a poem titled 'Twa Warlds' and followed it with the other thirty poems which make up 'In Place of Wark'. I print here a little group of poems from that sequence which have been admired by critics. My own favourites are 'Abstract Question', 'Fantasy' and 'Ageless Fourteen' although I am also attached to 'Twa Warlds' for the non-critical reason that it was the start of the sequence. In our hall hangs a photograph of Degas' 'The Little Dancer Aged Fourteen' and it is now about as much a favourite of mine as the first Degas I saw in my boyhood in the Glasgow Art Gallery which is of a man sitting in front of a wall of books. It is mentioned in one of my poems but not by name although I know it to be a portrait of Edmond Duranty.

II

CONCRETE CRITICISM

I look at Matisse's 'Reading Woman with
Parasol' and think

why does her elbow no slip aff the table?

III

TWA WARLDS

I sit in my moulded black chair
near to Matisse's 'Draped Nude' (1936).

Sometimes someane touches a canvas
and I staun up, which is usually enough.
I'm no a man o unnecessary words.

Sometimes I adjust the thermostat.
Sometimes tak a daunder round the gaillery
and if it's empty staun by my favourite wark.
It's Henri Matisse's 'Draped Nude'
by the door.
Next to it is his 'The Inattentive Reader' (1919)
bequeathed by M. Shearman
through the Contemporary Art Society 1940.
No.5141.

I'm especially fond o its frame
wi decoratit gilt in twa layers
gien a wee sunken ledge at the tap
atween its back and front.
There I keep my baa-point pen.

XVI

ABSTRACT QUESTION

I see Jackson Pollock's
'Untitled (Yellow Islands)' (1952).

Is it Bahamas
or Bananas?

XVII

SELF-PORTRAIT

There in Philadelphia tae
I stood afore a young man
facin life erect and square on.

The Iberian barbarism in the heid,
massive, solid torso
and haimmer-like haund.

A human being sad
and visionary
but the heid held up wi wide-open een
and a look made to last
in aa its confident gentleness . . .

Pablo Picasso, 'Self-Portrait' (1906)

XVIII

FANTASY

Sometimes I feel as if I could slip in
at the edges o ane or twa paintins.

Mebbe float doun aside Marc Chagall
in 'The Poet Reclining'
and hae my moment as pairt
o his honeymoon wi the faithfu Bella.
Mebbe visit his house at Vitebsk
and gaither little white flouers
as the cock crows in the first licht.
And float in the clear blue sky owreheid
afore sclimin up owre baith husband and wife's
shoulders to mak a triple portrait
wi twa wine glasses raised heich
celebratin the joy o Bella and Marc
triumphant in luve. Or mebbe
an orange donkey in my een
jinin in the flicht o joy
on Bella's Birthday. Be a second green violinist
sittin on a stool astride twa houses
and bigger than the village
serenadin the haill fantastic warld.

Or in ither mood lift Dali's telephone
frae his beach scene and say
what *I* think!

XIX

IMOOS?

Dae you ken IMOOS? A rare moose
frae northern climes near extinct?
Imitator o coos?
Or UFO's distant kin?

It is baith Op and kinetic and mebbe nou Pop.
It is baith mechanical and illusionistic.
It's here trapped in a gaillery. A complex
o rotatin forms
afore a concave mirror, maist obviously
makin you think o Cubism
– if you hae read the books.

But IMOOS? Weill nou . . .
and here and then . . .
and there . . .

*I*mages *M*oving *O*ut *O*nto *S*pace!

XX

AGELESS FOURTEEN

I stop by Degas'
'The Little Dancer Aged Fourteen'
sae superior, sae beautiful in her pose
wi haunds joyfully cupped ahint her back.
As aye I notice the fadit cloth o her skirt
and the tattered ribbons tyin her hair.
I wonder if they'll renew them
to match her eternal youth
wondrously caught in bronze.

CHAPTER 28

Of Two Men

THE POEM 'Poet's Gairden Gnome' which I quoted in a previous chapter is a kind of humorous 'In Memoriam' poem to myself, but within sixteen months of our move to Radcliffe-on-Trent on 28th April 1978 two people very important to me had died – Christopher Grieve or Hugh MacDiarmid on 9th September 1978 and my father on 27th August 1979. I heard the news of MacDiarmid's death from my mother who was visiting us with my father at the time. She heard it on the radio and came out to the garden where I was sitting in the sun to tell me. I was most upset and not too polite to her.

Quite a lot of people phoned me to ask me to write on MacDiarmid but I refused them all and, indeed, found it difficult to speak to them. Part of an essay I wrote for the first MacDiarmid double issue of *Akros* was reprinted (with acknowledgment that it was a reprint) in the Welsh magazine *Planet* in November 1978. Later I was asked several times to talk on MacDiarmid but again I refused except for one lecture in Cardiff on 3rd December 1978. Even for my 'In Memoriam' piece in *Akros* 39 (December 1978) I confined myself to three lines of prose: 'This issue of *Akros* has been extended by the death of Christopher Murray Grieve. Sadness is all and words are inadequate except the words of Christopher Grieve himself.' There then followed an 'In Memoriam' section which comprised two portrait drawings by Leonard Penrice from *Poems Addressed to Hugh MacDiarmid* and many quotations from MacDiarmid's prose and poetry – the prose introducing or linking the poetry. I had used a similar mixture of prose and poetry in a long radio programme I compiled for MacDiarmid's seventy-fifth birthday. How happily active I was to celebrate that birthday in 1967 and indeed continued to be active until his eighty-fifth birthday.

In 1967 in addition to *Poems Addressed to Hugh MacDiarmid* and the radio programme I proposed an exhibition at the National Library of Scotland as tribute to the poet. The Library put a big effort into this exhibition and I was pleased to help with advice although when the catalogue appeared I did not know whether to be flattered or angry at the extensive use of my researched facts from *Hugh MacDiarmid and the Scottish Renaissance* over which I laboured long. I tried to get Ezra Pound contacted to write a preface to the catalogue but in the end R. S.

Thomas wrote it. In a letter of 3rd August 1967 MacDiarmid wrote to me of the opening of the exhibition, 'I think the thing went off very well, and the Catalogue was excellently done – especially Rev. R. S. Thomas's preface.'

Earlier in July of that year, as I have said, I had got *On a Raised Beach* into separate publication through the Harris Press, Preston. It is interesting to me to find Ruth McQuillan movingly writing in her essay '*Akros* and Schiehallion. Scottish Poetry as I See It 1965-1981' in *Akros* 50 (October 1982): 'think on a time no juist canny but no lang syne when it was ill to find "On a Raised Beach". I hae number 54 of the Harris Press imprentit of yon poem. Hugh MacDiarmid gied it til me his self the third of April 1969, whilk was the first time I was at Candymill. Then siccan a visit was pairt of life. And nou? History blawn by the wind past the deid fire in a tuim chaulmer. It maun be a bad sign (for me, likely no for Scots poetry) when yon dearth at the hairt of things gars the past mair til me as present or future ever can be.'

In November 1969, as I have said, Cape published MacDiarmid's *Selected Essays* edited by me and in April 1970 I published the first MacDiarmid double issue of *Akros*. August 1971 saw the publication by Gollancz of the collection of essays *Whither Scotland?* which I edited as a contribution to the debate on the new emerging Scotland. In fact the book was just too early and although very extensively reviewed was remaindered although later books rather like it sold very well when devolution for Scotland (and Wales) had become West-minster issues. *Whither Scotland?* has a long essay by MacDiarmid over which, as his letters to me show, he took much care despite his advancing years. There was, however, one scare as he explained in a letter to me dated 8th June 1970: 'The essay for "Whither Scotland?" ought to have been in your hands a week ago and would have been but for a mishap. One of my bags went amissing and I have just recovered it. Needless to say it contained my notes and other material for the essay and lack of these brought me to a standstill.' If only men a quarter of his age were so concerned to meet deadlines! And so considerate and polite in correspondence. According to a count made by the National Library of Scotland when I deposited the letters there in 1978 I received 127 most civilised letters from Christopher Grieve between 1962 and 1977 although I received two letters in 1978 so the count may not be quite complete.

My involvement with MacDiarmid continued with the publication in 1972 by Scottish Academic Press of *Hugh MacDiarmid. A Critical Survey*. In August 1977, to jump ahead, I published a special second MacDiarmid double issue of *Akros* to celebrate the poet's 85th birth-day. This gave him much pleasure from what he said to me when I met

him in Edinburgh after an international conference on his poetry
organised by Tom Nairn and at which I acted as chairman. In a letter to
me of 7th August 1977 MacDiarmid wrote of an essay I had written for
his birthday as being, with Edwin Morgan's essay in the Longman's
'Writers and their Work' series, 'excellent, and the special issue of
Akros with Coia's drawings is a wonderful bonus. Even with Arts
Council support I don't know how you manage it.'

When I left Preston Polytechnic in 1978 the staff there kindly produced a festschrift for presentation to me entitled *Our Duncan Who
Art in Trent . . .* and Philip Pacey who edited it asked, without my
knowledge, MacDiarmid to contribute to it. On 15th February 1978 I
received a most kind and modest and wonderful letter from a dread-
fully ill Christopher Grieve explaining and apologising for not being fit
enough to contribute to the festschrift. I shall always treasure it as not
only one of the last but also one of the kindest letters I received from a
truly great man.

So, having been so involved with Christopher Grieve so long in so
many ways it may seem strange that I backed away from paying
tributes to him on his death but it meant too much to me. I still mourn
for Christopher Grieve. About 1980 I had the idea that I would like to
write an 'In Memoriam' poem for MacDiarmid but the words did not
come until May 1983 when I wrote the twenty-six poem sequence 'In
Memoriam Hugh MacDiarmid' from which I have already quoted the
second section. As tribute to MacDiarmid I quoted sections from it in
my editorial to the last *Akros* but here I would quote the sections that
Bill Herbert printed in the first number of *The Gairfish* where he also
kindly described the whole sequence as 'Duncan Glen's important new
elegaic sequence to MacDiarmid'.

III

Border life raw,
vigorous, rich, bawdy, braw
and burstin wi life and gusto ilka day
as you sae fairly say.

A near tropical scene
of Nature. And you keen
on great forests and honey-scentit heather hill.
And takin mony and mony a time your fill
on the Langfall when the hines were ripe and een,
shinin ahint leaves, seen
wi the joy o youth. And moorlands rife
wi little-kent flouers, wi animal and insect life,
and aa around ayont ony human strife
the subtle relationships of watter and life.

And a multitude of rivers
each wi its distinct music.

The true test of your wark, being what you sought to dae
the measure it has caught, you say,
that unquenchable Border humour locked
to bitin satire soaked
in profound wisdom cloaked in banterin gaiety.
The wealth of wud humour ayont aa fears
or thocht of tears
in licht-hairtit, reckless assault
on and on without a halt
upon the conventions of dull respectability.

V

I can put in aathing as you ask yoursel.
Bend to the task again and again being mysel
Riskin landin up aneath the tramplin geese.
And yet sun on the sheep's fleece.

Being at ane wi aa, you say. A haill land,
A haill people ilka day. I throw the sand
Agin the wund and walk into it.
The labours of aa that is me as I sit only sit.

Put in aathing as you ask yoursel. The bairn at school.
Intellectual boxin up his ideas. The fool
Playin at it. Man diggin the ditches.
And daurk-suitit banker at his desk rationin out riches.

Men ploughin fields. Auld ladies
Sellin sweets. Wha doun in Hades?
Border mill-warkers and steelmen by Clyde.
The aipple-pie I had for dinner, as an aside.

Merlin complainin unner his muckle rock.
And me sat by your stane as I tak stock.

VI

Abyss is
The element where,
Where this is
Everywhere.

Flung into it
He sings
To a ticht fit
And sprouts wings.

Hou heich you flee
Out of the abyss.
Nou see
This this?

VII

Like Jacob Boehme
on a green afore
Neys Gate at Goerlitz
in 1600

viewin the herbs and gress

you see into their essences
use
and properties

suddenly

as Boehme's
spirit did brak
through

e'en into the innermost birth
of Geniture of the Deity

and there was embraced in luve
as bridegroom
embraces
his beloved bride.

VIII

Imagination
Comin to get us into reality.
Into existence we shun
No faur enough out or in or doun.
But there we hope to be soon.
'Are you Nobody?' asks Emily Dickinson.
'Dae you ken silence?' you ask, Hugh.
Is it time to gie up douts?
To get doun to the task owredue?
There are twa great pouers says Johannes v Muller,
Round which aa revolves and flouers.
'I hae questionin doubts.
And I can't be satisfied.'
'I've got the sense to care twa hoots
And I can't be satisfied.'
Johannes v Muller I question
But for sure canna shun.

The twa great pouers, the tempters
Into existence, women and ideas. What deters?
Thousands run efter a skirt. Oohs and aahs!
But amang them aa, wha moved by ideas?

X

Beatin a rhythm out agin the storm,
Thinkin claps of thunder in new form.
    I hear you shout
Up agin the sma minds ilka day and nicht.
I see you sat aneath the lift heavy wi grey and yella licht.
    What's it aa about?
    What's it aa about?
Genius like a thunder-storm
Which comes up against the wund. A conflagration
Which the storm challenges black afore the sun.
    Storm! Storm!
You movin to and fro agin the sma minds
Wha sing the sma tuneless ditties of their kinds.

I have, of course, written poems involving my father. I have already quoted 'My Faither' but *The Turn of the Earth* has poems involving my father which were written in Radcliffe-on-Trent in April 1983 including this poem:

SUNNY DAY

Very auld
he stauns in his gairden
wi the sun ahint him.

He's near translucent.

Can I see richt
through him?

He doesnae ken I'm there.

I concentrate on his richt
ear. It glows wi licht
shinin through
but nocht is seen

through it

till he turns to me
wi a smile

and a pull
at his ear.

For my father I have been able also to write an 'In Memoriam'
poem. I was very pleased to have it first printed separately in *Lines
Review*, No. 71, March 1980, but it is part of *On Midsummer Evenin
Merriest of Nichts?* I print it without comment.

I hear the voice o my faither
deein in hospital bed.
I think on his flouers and plants.
But maistly flouers . . .

Sad the thocht of his flouers, yet joy.
Each Summer through his sixties
and into his mid-seventies
he comes to us wi flouers large and sma.

Flouers transplantit twa hundrit miles
wrappt ticht in wet moss
and kept out the bus's luggage boot
for their care and protection.

Efter tea he oversees their plantin
guidin Margaret's haunds ye feel
for aa he stauns sae still and upricht
and nae word says, though weill pleased.

He sees we watter them each nicht
for the fortnicht he is wi us
and leaves nae doubt we're to continue
when he's back in his ain gairden.

Plants he tendit aa the Winter and Spring
and flourishin in their native sile.
Flouers frae the reid sandy sile o Ayrshire
to the heavy grey clay o Lancashire.

And soon they die but he is back next year
wi flouers large and sma.

Hou at seventy-fowre he talks
and puts aff dyin
wi joy in his mither near reachin ninety.

The short days in the greenhouse
pottin young plants
to await the lang Summer time.

And new daffodil bulbs plantit
juist to the richt depth
for the next year's Spring to come.

Selfish but kind and wise
he weeds his gairden
and mony flouers are in bloom.

Hou at echty-five his mither still spry
and taen by surprise at ninety
when expectin a hundrit years
and a telegram frae the Queen.

Hou at seventy-five he walks gey stechie
wi dizzy steps and rubber-endit stick.
He seems hauf his size
a new suit owre, owre big.

And us nou in Nottingham
and large Victorian house
he gets lost in. Yet flouers he brings
as aye, if anither fremit gairden.

Hou he talks wi weariness of his mither
young at his auld age
and mony plants no pottit this year
in a neglectit greenhouse.

It is July and he is seventy-six.
I walk round his gairden and pick flouers
growein near wild
for his bedside.

I dig his empty vegetable plots
and turn in knee-high weeds.
I report my progress in his pride and joy
but he's got thochts only for himsel
and for us
and for the day.

I leave him to his rest or thochts
and walk again slawly, slawly round
                    a lonely, lonely garden.
The greenhouse stauns bare.

I sclim the hill to the hospital
wi a bunch o flouers frae his gairden.

He's in a room by himsel
but recognises me wi tears.
He'd thocht I wisnae comin.
His watch had stoppt that mornin
or the nicht afore
at nine o'clock without his kennin.
He thocht it past the evenin visitin 'ours.

For the first and last time
I wound his watch.

And leave him wi his flouers . . .

CHAPTER 29

I Am Quite Alane

I HAVE already written of my sense of history and my sense of being one of a long line of poets of the Scots tradition but as I have already said in referring to my poem 'Poet' and in introducing the river section of *Mr & Mrs J. L. Stoddart at Home* often, like most human beings, have the sense of standing alone. Someone, was it Yeats?, said there were only two major subjects for a poet, love and death. Most people must feel alone when facing death and my poems on death certainly reveal this sense of isolation. There is a death section in my *On Midsummer Evenin Merriest of Nichts?* and the first line reads 'I am quite alane'. This section was first printed in *Chapman* (23-24, Spring 1979) under the title 'This Ae Nicht'. Writing of it, as it was printed in *On Midsummer Evenin Merriest of Nichts?* in *Lines Review* (No. 80, March 1982) Donald Campbell described it as 'the most powerful section of the poem . . . in which the poet imagines himself on his death bed. The dangers inherent in such a poetic gambit are obvious, but Glen brings it off faultlessly, with total conviction and not even the slightest hint of bathos. Such an exercise is, I think, typical of Duncan Glen, who is a poet who has never been afraid to take risks in his work. In his own, highly individual use of Scots, in his espousal of complicated and difficult themes, in his austere, often stiff-necked assertion of his own poetic philosophy, he has never sought to be "kent like Pam Ayres on TV", but rather has tried to "make it new" more completely than any of his contemporaries.'

I AM QUITE ALANE

I am quite alane.
The sma 'ours surround me.
Am I passin frae life to daith?
I am without priest.
I am without Christ.
Or passin frae daith to life?
Without freens.
Without feres.
Without allies.
Without sympathy.
Without luve.
Alane.

I lie alane in the nicht
ticht in this last bed
and wait for what will be
or will no be.
Wha hear my final words?
Wha can I say goodbye to
at this late 'our?
What haund touch?

Am I gaein to jine my freens
in a warld of licht?
Or am I richt to fear the daurk?
The switch o kennin and being
flicked aff
and that deid wecht through that door
aa that was me.
Surely an end without fear?

Desolate I would turn to the waa,
pull the sheets ticht round me
and be ended.
But aa will and strength has gone.
I lie cauld
immovable
fearfully alane
in my mind.

What of Hell?
The lang time of neither eternal life and luve
nor naethingness.
Self-condemned by thrawnness
as Dante's eternal spirits.
Will I be my ain creator of hell
asides being in Hell?
A hell frae which there is nae escape
for aa a desire for the licht
to be quite out
ayont fear and tremblin.

Alane in this hospital bed
at the end of the warld's line
I feel my sides touch padded box
and draw my airms ticht to my body.
I wunner if I'll outlast the paddin
till I think of my juices
soakin through.

In this hauf-daurk warld
I think the Pauline thocht

'I shall be known as I shall be shown'.
But there's Lazarus tae
stinkin to nae heivan it seems
alane, alienated, isolatit,
perishin.
And yet aa a question-merk
to me
waitin, waitin
alane in this hauf-licht warld
for a haund to touch me
in luve.

Why should I live for ever?
I think of the boredom of eternal existence.
I think of the lack of flesh
and of you my luve.
I think. I think, I think
as a young man.
Nou I lie in this tail-end bed
and fear gaein out thae swingin doors.

Thochts, thochts, thochts
polemics of our sma sels
our sma faimily
our sma civilisation.
I cry out in memory of luve
exchanged
and aa is licht and sound
in harmony
eternally.

I think o Jeans
sayin that the warld is mair like
great thocht
than great machine. Here
at this last end
I'm aa thocht
whether fear or joy or luve.
I am at peace
and ane wi the world
– till again I feel thae paddit sides
and hear thae swingin doors.

Why are they no pleyin Mozart
or Bach loud in this ward
to help me cross the unkent line
and gie me hope of heivan?'You are with me'
is the cry
and I hear Pauline words again

'Glory thou me, as I have glorified thee'.
But no priest to reassure me.
Christ an image of luve.

I lie cauld in a bed
at the end of the warld's line
and reach out for a haund
that has left.
I fear the end
mysel
alane.

Glory. Glory. Glory.
I sigh and reach for an orchestra
of sound in acceptance
'whosoever cares for his own safety is lost'.
Timeless and infinite I lie.
I forget thochts of the dawn
and of visitin 'ours
and touchin haunds.

'Glory thou me, as I have glorified thee.'

But hou I hope she comes aince mair to me
wi returnin luve
in touchin haunds . . .

CHAPTER 30

A New Harmony?

BY THE middle seventies, despite the occasional outbursts of controversialists or fighters or crusaders, the cultural climate in Scotland was more relaxed than it was in the late sixties and early seventies. There remains 'a new harmony' amongst the younger poets, or rather amongst the poets who emerged into some prominence in the seventies as some of them, including myself, are not now so young. I recognised this coming together in an essay 'A New Harmony? Younger Scottish Poets Today' in *Akros* 27, April 1975, in which I referred to quite a list of newish poets who were writing in Scots or English, or harmoniously in a mixture of both languages. Since then even more younger poets have received some recognition and they seem to be continuing the less aggressive attitudes shown by their immediate predecessors.

It has not been (and it is not) my intention in this book to assess critically the poetry of my own generation, or indeed that of any generation, but I would quote from the interview in *Akros* 50 (October 1982) in which I refer to some young poets for whom I have high hopes and who only began to attract editorial and critical attention towards the end of the seventies or even not until into the eighties. Speaking as editor of *Akros*, I said in reply to the question 'whom are you confident of?' in relation to recently emerged poets:

'D.G.: I am very hopeful of Raymond Vettese, Robert Crawford, Raymond Falconer and Christopher Rush.
M.I.: Which of them do you have highest hopes for?
D.G.: I don't think like that – it smacks of competitive gamesmanship. But I think Raymond Vettese has a vigour and a freshness of technique which could lead to important work. I think Robert Crawford is quite simply an astoundingly mature poet in technique and imaginative insight for one so young. Raymond Falconer's work I have admired for its control yet freedom since I first printed it in No. 26 (December 1974). And like many another before him in this century he was excited and thought he was really starting as a poet when he began to write in Scots early in 1981. Christopher Rush's work obviously shows excellent technical control and how high my hopes are for his work can be seen by how often I've printed it since he made his first appearance in No. 43 (April 1980).

M.I.:   But don't you think it is dangerous to over-encourage poets who have done very little?

D.G.:   Maybe, but when I see a young poet with as much natural talent as Robert Crawford I think it only right to say that that is what I think. That young man can really take the breath away.

M.I.:   But...

D.G.:   But there are plenty of other hopefuls I could name, not least some like Bill Brown, Rob King and George Gunn who have not appeared in *Akros*. Or like Geddes Thomson who has appeared only once I think. And there are, of course, also all the more established poets who have appeared in the sixties and seventies.'

It does seem, as Jeremy Hooker said of poets who emerged in the seventies that their work does show 'that Scottish poetry deserves to enjoy an atmosphere of excited confidence'. He went on to say that the confidence of these poets 'is, in part at least, a confidence in Scotland' and that is something that has perhaps changed in the eighties. The new harmony may generally remain, but some of the widespread optimism of even a few years ago seems to have gone into the post Devolution Referendum air. Indeed, in an essay 'The Survival of Scottish Literature' in *Akros* 50, October 1982, Donald Campbell wrote:

'Since the debacle of the Devolution Referendum in 1979, Scotland has been engulfed by a great tidal wave of provincialism. The political, social and artistic fires which burned so brightly in the seventies have now, it seems, been well and truly doused and a gigantic wet blanket covers the entire country. The disastrous result of the Referendum may have been brought about by a piece of blatant political chicanery, but its overall effect has had repercussions which transcend the political arena. The fact that Scotland does not now have her own Assembly is much less important, *in this particular respect*, than the fact that the majority of the Scottish electorate voted *in favour* of such an Assembly. Even the notorious 40% rule, so fiercely debated at the time, can now be seen to have been, after all, quite irrelevant to the central truth of the matter – namely, that Westminster was able to sweep the wishes of the Scottish people aside, with complete and absolute impunity. The result of the Referendum re-emphasised Scotland's powerlessness, underlined our insignificance as a nation. The resulting trauma has sent shock waves through the Scottish consciousness, leaving all our national aspirations in splinters. Literature has felt the effect of this sickening loss of morale as much as any other area of Scottish life.'

But Donald Campbell agrees with me on the new harmony of the seventies. He writes:

'There are, of course, a great many ways of "being Scottish". One of the great gains of the seventies, it seems to me, was that the great upsurge of literary activity which took place during the course of the decade was accompanied by creation of a much more tolerant atmosphere in literary circles. The prejudices and petty hatreds which were so much in evidence at the end of the sixties have, as a result, been greatly reduced. The proliferation of magazines and publications of all kinds, plus the growth of the poetry-reading movement, had the effect of bringing Scottish writers together, giving them a degree of artistic and social contact that had hardly been possible in the previous decades. With such a healthy atmosphere prevailing, the temptation to take up entrenched positions has all but disappeared and one can discern, in the work of the younger writers, a certain readiness to face, without any sense of artistic insecurity, the bitter realities of life in Scotland today. Despite all its difficulties, Scottish Literature continues to move forward in all sorts of directions.'

Donald Campbell contrasts very usefully the approach of two young poets – Raymond Vettese and George Gunn – concluding:

'The differences which are discernible in the work of these two young poets add up to something that is a cause for celebration – but the important fact is, I think, that we are fast reaching a point where such a situation will be too obvious to need stating. Ten years ago, Vettese and Gunn might have found themselves on opposite sides of some squalid literary argument about language or nationalism or some such, but nobody much cares about such bickering now and the two poets can be seen as elements in a spectrum which includes a great many others: Andrew Greig, Ron Butlin, Brian McCabe, Jim Campbell, Liz Lochhead, Walter Perrie, Kathleen Jamie; older poets like Tom Leonard, Alastair Mackie, Duncan Glen, Stewart Conn, Douglas Dunn, Iain Crichton Smith; and even older poets like Alexander Scott, Edwin Morgan, Maurice Lindsay, George Bruce and Norman MacCaig. Scottish poetry is really in excellent condition, more than equal to the very considerable difficulties that will have to be faced in the eighties. Although many of these difficulties will be of an economic nature – the fact has to be faced that the tolerance of the seventies was very largely the result of increased Arts Council support – it should be remembered that the squabbles of the past had their origins in a certain absence of goodwill, created by a starvation of opportunity. Irrespective of the financial difficulties, we should never allow such a situation to occur again.'

In 1983 my long poem *The State of Scotland* was published and although I hope that basically, with its references not only to Scotland but also to international influences, it is an optimistic work, I do also reveal in it fears of destructive influences at work. But I see Scotland and events of the poem set in a potentially creative situation. A situation based on 'the private turn of events/destined to boom later/ like gowden chimes', on 'local personal roots/to raise blossoms owre aa the warld' and on 'the certain local roots/for global flouers'. So I put my faith ultimately in the personal and the local and, as did Carlos Williams, in the particular from which rises the universal in literature.

> But let us stert again
> out of particulars
> thinkin of William Carlos Williams
> true to his native grund.
>
> Doctor Williams
> hou mony babies did you bring
> into the warld? Hou much
> poverty and disease did you see
> in Rutherford?
>
> Yes Paterson 'lies in the valley
> under the Passaic Falls'
> as we mak a stert out of particulars.
> And my Cambuslang
> lies by the ripplin, wimplin weys of Clyde
> bricht on simmer's day
> but anither Rutherford
> in the auld Europe.
> And is my present and past. Yet the past
> is for those of the past for aa that
> memory is 'a sort of renewal'.
>
> 'Yah! Yah! Yah! Yah!'
> 'Bow, wow! Bow, wow!'
>
> And you Dr Williams
> still in your pants, coat and vest?
> And 'geeze, Doc, I guess it's all right
> but what the hell does it mean?'
> Dear Doctor Williams,
> hou mony babies did you bring
> into the warld
> new born
> amang the words?

But this start out of particulars involves, as I have said, the destructive elements although the devouring rats of *The State of Scotland* in my grandfather's particular steading are also part of the rich variety of life.

Again I mak a stert
out of particulars.

In the fairmyaird of my grandfaither
the autumn moon shines
bricht and white. Lang,
hidin shadows faa outwards
frae the steading. And round aa
a silence
toom as the house's daurk windaes.

I gae into the piggery
and snap on licht. Mice scamper
but rottin there, its een
starin straucht at me. I advance
and still he would haud his grund.
I punch fist haurd into haund. He's aff.

He's quick alang beam
abune the sty. Gone
wi rustle o straw into his daurk warld.
The mice run again and single pig
grunts as I advance doun
the wet passage.
Ither rottin stares.

Soon he's gone tae but aa still there
wi devourin, frenzied greed.
And life to be drawn
in the warm daurkness
frae heich-stacked sacks of gowden grain
and aged timbers
supportin the auld house.

The icy wund whines
out of the daurkness.

But I am an optimist and see in *The State of Scotland* our country
made independent, creative and civilised. As I sing towards the end of
the poem:

This joyfu day
I see the sunlicht
brak through and shine bricht
owre aa the land till ayont sicht
ray efter ray.

The gairden skinklin wi colour
frae mony single blooms
creatin bed efter bed.

And a peel of celebratory bells
ower aa the land
that is the new Scotland.
A gowden boom frae heich touer
heard round aa the warld.

A gairden nou fillin
aa the stage
alive wi native flouers
makin new form
yet fed by auld roots
and aa the warld
that is.

A gairden soarin as cathedral.

But perhaps we should not be over-optimistic about a continuation of the new harmony even in literary matters. People will always fight for their beliefs and those who take intellectual stances, including those relating to the theory of poetry, are as good or as bad at it as any other group of individuals. I expressed this in a poem in *In Appearances:*

WEE BOXES

Intellectuals
we walk apairt and staun wi oursels.
Watter-ticht logic
in boxes we command
wi an ee for justice to the idea.

The battle o the Somme.
The British deid.
The twenty-thousand on the day.

For ideas we hae isolation blocks
– maximum security. Haigs awa frae hospitals
or the clearin stations.

We hae our ideas and justice
seen to be done
wi belief for baurs.

Ane million deid
and Haig wi the courage to command.

As can be expected from my record as an editor and theorist of poetry, I wish the young poets, who will emerge with new ideas and practices, well and hope they do not have to fight too many spokesmen for authoritarian forces who will defend their own against the new. Long may the new harmony continue, but who is to say that the Scottish literary community will in the long term be any more successful than most other human groups in throwing off aggressive tendencies. When authoritarians encounter foreign dolls – whether in person or as ideas – they often attempt to pull them to pieces. This is an idea I have expressed in a poem in *In Appearances:*

DRESST TO KILL

We're dresst to kill.
It's a white tie and tails affair.

There's nae bare breists here.
Nae drinkin frae the finger bowl.

Aa's talk and polisht siller.
We ken the ceremony.

We staun in lines wi pride in our weys.
We toast our peers – our heids thrown back.

Let in the lang-haired ane.
Let her roll naukit on the table.
Bring in the scabby heid.
The hairy-breastit ane.
The ane-leggit dwarf.

The stiff protectin fronts are burst.
Thocht's broken doun wi its sophistication.
Reid-breistit emotion's in the drivin seat.
Aa's nuclear pouer and lynch-mob gane wud.

We're faur ayont ony chimps' tea-pairty.
We'll tear the stuffin out ony fremit doll.

But being by nature an optimist, I would not wish to end this chapter on harmony on that somewhat pessimistic note and will end instead by quoting a section from *On Midsummer Evenin Merriest of Nichts?* which begins lightly or humorously but ends with what are I hope five serious lines on some of the foundations of the creative act which is the hopeful outcome of a new harmony in Scottish culture: there is no sense in a cultural harmony if it does not lead to works of art:

Wha unnerstauns
this gemm of poetry?

Wha unnerstauns poets?

Poets unnerstaun poets.
I am a poet. I am a poet.
I am a poet. I am a poet.

Critics unnerstaun poets.
Better deid.

Poets unnerstaun poets.
Of mysel . . .

Wha unnerstauns art?
Whaur its foundations?

As a bairn I kicked mony a stane
alang mony grey streets. Or tin can.
As a man I liftit mony a stane
as object trouvé. Or battered tin can.
Or bairn heid doun alang a grey street.

Display case at the Akros Exhibition at the National Library of Scotland

CHAPTER 31

On Correspondences

As I HAVE already said, I have not socialised with Scottish poets perhaps as much as might be expected. This lack of personal contact was both an advantage and a disadvantage to me as editor of *Akros* and as a publisher of books. Obviously I could miss ideas through not mixing daily with Scottish writers but on the other hand I did not get taken over by cliques formed on a personal basis. But many people have come to visit me and when I lived in Preston I went regularly to Edinburgh. But my real contact with other poets not only in Scotland but around the world has been by correspondence. My personal correspondence with a wide variety of individuals has been one of my joys. In the sixties and seventies Alastair Mackie and I exchanged letters weekly and I have also done this with others including Nigel Thompson when he was living as curator in the Brownings' house in Florence. Currently the two poets with whom I am in regular correspondence are Margaret Gillies and Bill Herbert. The former lives in a farmhouse in Perthshire near the Tay; the latter is a post-graduate student at Oxford. As letter writers they make a fine contrast but what they have in common is a full commitment to poetry. I am most grateful to all those poets and others who have written to me personally. The National Library of Scotland has a huge holding of the correspondence to me and I think it shows very often the generosity of so many people towards me and their other contemporaries. Whilst I have been writing to Margaret Gillies her husband, Ronald, died and I sent her a poem addressed to her soon after his death. I have since absorbed it into my sequence *The Stones of Time* in which context I sent it to Bill Herbert who kindly thought it one of the poems he liked best in the sequence. I print it in this book as tribute to a brave woman and to mark my appreciation of her correspondence to me and also the correspondence of the many, many others who have written to me.

TO MARGARET GILLIES
(of East Inchmichael)
IN MEMORY OF RONALD GILLIES
FEBRUARY 1924 – DECEMBER 1982

This your lowest time
the sun pale and weak.

221

An eternity of timeless sadness and pain-shairp sorrow,
and aa extendit in memories that aince were joy and warmth.
        Your despairin time
            aneath a grey sky
growein daurk early and yet adorned wi mindit staurs
that highlicht this sad time's daurk clouds.

Frae you I ken a man that preserved his weys
            e'en agin winter's deep drifts;
he wore his views wi firmness yet set in reality
of stillness and gentleness. He murmurs a few strong words
extendit by guid sound sense. There is much joy in his authority
            and in his movements.

Theday your hills hae nae rich greenness
            nae delichtfu warmth of summer sun.
There are nae heich hills it seems to be sclimed
in this time of low sun and lang shadows.
But memories of gowden sunset reflectin on sheep-fleece
            for aa presently addin to the greyness aa around.

I see your fairmyaird geese sittin like rocks
            ignorin the stormy weather
wi juist a quirk of stylish necks or slaw look round;
the storm blaws aa around but for them nae goose steps
to the shelter of barn. You see them flet-based boats
            moored and barely rockin.

I see your disused sawmill, deserted it seems,
            a buildin made of stane but crumlin a little.
Yet the lark sings owreheid, if alane;
a strayin sheep steps out the open door
and wild flouers tak owre aa around
            in this place aince full of human vigour.

            And aside the mill chiselled statue
                weatherin mony winter's blast.
A creation by ane wha loved strong-limbed folk
walkin the fithills and sclimin our heich bens.
            A strong symbol
                raised against the sky,
kennin time would pass and sawmill be left,
yet rejoicin for what we create wi love.

I see your disused sawmill and chiselled statue
            daurk nou on winter's nicht
but memorial to those that were
and are frae the seein ee and sensed word.
Images of continuity and mebbe eternity livin on
            in creative acts of life and leid.

He promised you nae roses
    when you were young and first in love.
Him wise as auld houses, you say. Your house that smiles and says
naethin. You accepted that winter's snaws hide the flouers.
    But soon there's snaw-in-summer
    coverin the base of sun-dial
that minds you of mony happy times
for aa a shadow nou faas across that gairden full of roses.

In the middle of the deluge you ask
    'Will my bridges hold?'
And I see you in time walkin again through your acceptin lichgate
to find yoursel again in summer gairden.
A gairden whaur it is warm, warm as winter turns
    to quiet and peacefu Spring.

And summer and autumn hairst-time to follow.
    I see you walkin wi straucht back
towards auld fields that glow wi separate fires.
It is again the time of straw-burnin at nicht-faa.
I see you bend a bunch of winnowed straw
    and licht it as torch

settin aff again myriad sparks of life, orange, yellow, red.
    Heat, energy and consumin licht owre the land
for aa you ken the flames maun dee
and aa for a time be burnt out owre the fields.
But through the simmerin haze the full hairvest moon
    rises calm and steidy as aye owre the horizon.

    But for nou it is your lowest time,
    the sun weak and pale
and fullest moon shut out ahint daurk clouds
as the brichtest staurs of past and present.
    Your despairin time
    in a festive season
set still in the hairts of lovin generations of faimily.
Yet the loss owrepourin as it maun be.

Joyfu birth of Jesus, your pure faith in child,
    announces there is hope.
Bethlehem wi ither stable and ither beasts.
The guid shepherds to be celebratit, the wise men, the joyfu
Christ and Mary. And become trust frae which aa rises again
    in a faith ayont ony kent leid.

    And you hae written
    of an upper room,
the table laid for twelve plus one,
and kent that room but yesterday for you.

And ae mornin kennin
a stirrin in your daurkness.
A pushin out of green, green shoots for the sunlicht
and themorrow's Easter.

Note: throughout this poem I have drawn on images and, indeed, words from
my memory of poems by Margaret Gillies.

Mrs Margaret Glen.

CHAPTER 32

Out of the Thick Daurkness

IN THIS book I have suggested various geographical situations which have been powerful in my imagination: the meeting of industrial and pastoral Lanarkshire; the burn on the Campsie Hills; our Penwortham garden, and so on. In the final line of the quotation which ended an earlier chapter, I lift up, as it were, myself as a 'bairn heid doun alang a grey street' and one's memory of self can be as important as memory of other people. So people can be as important, obviously, to creative ideas as geographical situations. As will be evident from this book, a recurring 'image' of my work, if I may so describe her, has been my wife. She has obviously been one of the inspirations of my life and work and quite soon after we moved to Radcliffe-on-Trent I began to write again poems inspired by her. I would like, being very near the end of this book, to quote one of them from *The Turn of the Earth*. It is one that pleases and amuses my wife and it reads:

BROWN MOUSE

You and I thegither.

She said you were brown mouse
your friend.

Brown blouse, brown skirt, brown shoes,
brown you in her house.

For sure if you wore a hat
it would be elegantly brown
sat atop your brown head.

And you hae summer tan being what you are
in the sun cool as a fan.

I see your broun een shine,
as mine, funny broun mouse

in our house

you and I
thegither.

But poems come essentially from areas beyond all obvious geographical or personal or intellectual sources. They come from areas of our psyche of which we have little or no direct knowledge or understanding. We accept our vision from this area of understanding; we take what we are given. I say 'given' but we do need to have an attitude of mind ready to accept the given vision. Having such an ability to 'see' the 'vision' is perhaps what separates the poets from the mere manipulators of words. Perhaps, as my friend Philip Pacey said after quoting lines from Wordsworth, 'the artist's remembering plumbs deeper springs even of cosmic memory than we can easily conceive'. The lines quoted by Philip were the following famous ones from 'Ode: Intimations of Immortality':

> Our birth is but a sleep and a forgetting:The soul that rises
> with us, our life's Star,
> Hath had elsewhere its setting,
> And cometh from afar:
> Not in entire forgetfulness,
> And not in utter nakedness,
> But trailing clouds of glory do we come
> From God, who is our home:

Before my attention was drawn to Wordsworth's lines I had written a long poem which forms the final section of *The Turn of the Earth*, entitled 'Experience'; the poem is divided by quotations from the Bible and I would particularly point out one of these, from 2 Chronicles 6:1, which reads: 'Then said Solomon, the Lord hath said that he would dwell in the thick darkness'. I suppose the experience this poem is concerned with is breaking through that 'thick darkness' and making contact with the 'God' whom Wordsworth says 'is our home'. It is, I suppose, concerned with the mystical experience but its mysticism also takes strength, as I hope do all my writings, from a deep knowledge of human love. I end this book, as I ended the final issue of *Akros*, by printing 'Experience' which I hope expresses the joy and love I find in life.

EXPERIENCE

And he said, Thou canst not see my face: for there shall be no man see me, and live.
EXODUS 33:20

> The birds chirp and sing
> and flee heich in the air.
> The sma animals scamper.
> The livin watter faas wi rich
> sound owre multi-colourt rocks.
> I smell the reek frae shepherd's cottage
> and see it couried doun
> in a fauld o the land.

Green sweyin trees are aa about.
E'en the wee bogs are a challenge this day.
Faur owreheid the sun shines doun
and the sky is blue aa around.
I hae wise, logical thochts
as I walk. I am at peace
and at ane wi aa that is.

I see in sherp images risin out
o that walk in the fithills
nou I'm middle-aged
wise wi logic and reason,
wi concepts,
wi ideas and images
and in full control o my technique
as a poem comes uncaad
frae the experiences o a lifetime's day.

To Hell wi it
I'm aff a fleein bird
into the daurk cloud
atap the heichest unkent ben. Here
aa is toom and cauld.
Aa is silence. My heid
birls ayont aa daily sense. I shut
my een and licht
ayont sicht
shines through me.
I caa on my luve o you
to raise me heicher still
in this warld o orchestratit
daurkness
and bricht silent music.

Then
I think.
Here
for sure's
anither poem.

And I'm flet on my middle-aged back
in fithill mire.

That the Lord called Samuel: and he answered, Here am *I.*
                                          1 SAMUEL 3:4

The mire hotches wi life
as I lie in the fithills
lie in the mire.

Lie in the mire, only lyin
and the wund moves the trees
and the gress growes green.

For I am with thee, saith the Lord, to deliver thee.
                                                      JEREMIAH 1:19

I lie still. At peace
ayont my daily sel.
A state of altered consciousness
I think and name.
But I leave the psychologists to their gemms
as I contemplate my image of peace.

I think of you
Lord God Almighty
my Father in Heaven
of my childhood.

Is this a state of grace?
Hae I been visitit by
the Holy Spirit
without faith
in thee o Lord?

Or reconciliation
about to be delivered?

As I lie safe
in my middle-age.

Woe unto him that striveth with his Maker!
                                                      ISAIAH 45:9

But I ask: 'Dae I believe in God?'
I flee aff a bird
that would chirp, chirp warnins
in thae fithills
agin that sleekit cat
low in the gress.

A cat still and quiet lang 'ours
yet alert to creep and leap
and strike
and throw playfully
frae paw to paw.
Nae bird but a mouse.

I ask: 'Hae you made me, Lord God
Almighty?'

And lie quiet and still
flet on my middle-aged back.

And sing in reply
as the storm braks
and thunder and lichtnin
near owreheid.

But risks hae to be taen
by singin makars
e'en in middle-age.

I rise to hide in the wud
believin thae trees
hae stood a lang time.

And he went out, not knowing whither he went.
HEBREWS 11:8

Forget warnin questionin
sangs. Forget gemms o the
psychologists
or gemms o leid
or reasonin theories
advancin. I thraw awa
my past
sae rich and alive in
my imagination. I need
nae support o
a future. I cling to nae
richts or wrangs. I'm in nae need
o 'Dae I believe in God?'

I gae I ken
not whaur. I am
free and feart,
streekit
in a terrible
daurk and toom silence.

I think
in fear.
I'll reach out for the sel,
to safe reason
and sensible thochts.

But I turn again.
I let gae aa that is me
into the daurk and toom
void.

The daurk is bricht as clearest sun
and the toomness
full wi aa that is

in joy.
I sense the great and singular
the essential essence
a tellin presence.

I contain aa that is

nou that I hae
nae need o them.

My God, my God, why has thou forsaken me? why art thou so
far from helping me, and from *the words of my roaring?*

PSALM 22:1

I lie atap a hill
streekit . . .
alane . . .

I shout faur back
agin the daurkness.
A roar rises to my lips
but silence passes
into the naethinness.

I'd kneel
if free
to see through the daurk cloud.
I'd staun
to cry agin the silence.

I lie back
into
the silence
and the daurkness . . .

Blue lochs are seen
pentit
on that heichest dome

and the white-tapped bens
to the ends of the earth.

Then said Solomon, the Lord hath said that he would dwell in the
thick darkness.

2 CHRONICLES 6:1

I lie wi you my luve.
My een are shut. Aa is
daurkness
that leads to you.
And the silence
broken only by leid ayont sense.

You and me thegither
our senses fully alive
ayont aa reason.

I hae said I mak
the Godheid
wi you
in this thick, divine
daurkness.

But dae I believe in God?

For sure I believe in you
and our luve.
I hae seen you
in baith licht and daurk.

'Hou could you see me
in the daurk?' you ask.

Mebbe I believe in God efter aa.

And Abraham stretched forth his hand, and took the knife to slay
his son.
                                        GENESIS 22:10

I walk the fithills
wi middle-aged stride.

I say I'm middle-aged. Quite true.
But what is fifty? Or sixty?
I think on the auld Abraham.

I'm aff atap that unkent ben.
I'm aff ayont aa that I ken.
I mak sacrifice
as I gae.

Sae I say
lichtly nou
kennin
it's aa safe in the mind

– till I faa owre the steep, steep edge
frae which there's nae return . . .

the spirit of knowledge and of the fear of the Lord:
                                        ISAIAH 11:2

I think of mysel
alive to you my luve.

I think.

I think of childhood fears
and the Lord God Almighty.

I think of daurk
cloud
and knowledge
ayont kennin.

I think of altered consciousness
I think of ego
of the unconscious personal to me
of the collective unconscious
of archetypes. I think ayont aa
that is named.

I think.

I think of mysel
atap that toomness
and ken it's surely me
drappin my daily sel
at wark there
in the daurk silence
deep in mysel.

I think of wudness
as the sel is lost ayont recall.

I think.
I think.

I think
I'll sit safe
on my middle-aged spread.

But I hope ayont fear
or thocht.
I trust to be aff again
a fleein bird
alive wi luve
ayont sel
into that daurk cloud
atap the heichest
unkent ben.

I accept luve out of the thick daurkness

I am in the joy and warmth
and bricht silent music
in that daurk cauld silence.

Index

INDEX   237

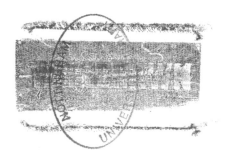